I can't think of a more eternally-sig
than the one Jesus asked Peter: 'Wh
can we find the answer to such a m
know that what we think about Je
knows that God's Word alone is wher
writing is faithful to Scripture, expertly organized, and worshipful.
This book is an excellent resource for anyone seeking to know
more about who Jesus is.

Gloria Furman

Author, *Treasuring Christ When Your Hands Are Full*

The doctrine of Christ is central to our understanding of the gospel
of grace and although many Christians know that, not many can
articulate why! This book will really help. Jenny Manley writes
with wisdom, clarity and conviction as she unpacks the person and
work of the Lord Jesus Christ and why our union with Him is so
important. But more than that, my heart was warmed as I read
about the Lord who suffered and died for me and not only wants
me to grow in my relationship with Him, but continues to apply the
benefits of His death to make it happen.

Carrie Sandom

Director of Women's Ministry, Cornhill Training Course,
Proclamation Trust, London

There is nothing more important for the life and health of the
church than to know Christ Jesus our Lord. Yet, sadly, faithful
biblical and theological teaching about the person and work of our
Lord Jesus is lacking in today's church, especially teaching written
for everyday followers of Christ. However, Jenny Manley has given
us a wonderful remedy to this problem in her excellent *The Doctrine
of Christ, for Every Woman*. In this careful biblical and theological study
of who Jesus is and what He has done for us, Jenny explains the
glory of the incarnation and the power and wisdom of the cross that
will serve the church well. If you want to grow in your knowledge,

love, and trust of Jesus, then this book is a must read. My hope is that it will be used in many churches so that women and men will become better equipped to proclaim Christ and the unsearchable riches of the Gospel.

Stephen J. Wellum
Professor, Christian Theology, Southern Baptist Theological Seminary,
Louisville, Kentucky

Jenny Manley, in this wonderfully clear book, reminds us about who Jesus is and what He has accomplished for us. Here we find biblically faithfully and theologically astute teaching about Jesus Christ, but at the same time the book is wonderfully clear and accessible. The book has another strength as well, for Manley shows us consistently why these truths about Jesus matter in our everyday lives. I rejoice to find a book about Jesus that is theologically profound and practically applicable which the ordinary person can understand.

Thomas R. Schreiner
James Buchanan Harrison Professor of New Testament Interpretation
and Associate Dean, The Southern Baptist Theological Seminary,
Louisville, Kentucky

Jenny Manley has produced a gift. This is a treasure trove of rich reflection on the most important figure in history. From beginning to end, Jenny uncovers the beauty and relevance of Christ's person and work. I know Jesus more truly, and love Him more deeply, because I read this book. Get two copies, read it with a friend, and marvel together at our King of glory.

Matt Smethurst
Managing editor, The Gospel Coalition
Author, *Before You Open Your Bible: Nine Heart Postures for Approaching God's Word*

Jenny Manley has picked on the choicest treasure in the stores of heaven to enrich the church on earth – Jesus Christ Himself. She writes primarily for women from the experience of one that has walked with Christ as a wife and mother and served Him both at home and on the mission field. Make no mistake about it, there is theology here – deep theology – but it is made easier to understand through anecdotes and study questions. You will be enriched by it!

Conrad Mbewe

Pastor, Kabwata Baptist Church, Lusaka, Zambia

Jesus Christ is the most glorious person you will ever know. The better you know Him the more you will love Him. Jenny Manley will help you know and worship Christ more as she draws the reader deep into the life and work of Christ. This book is full of deep theology and yet, it is an easy read as it stirs your heart and soul along with your mind. I recommend that every woman should read *The Doctrine of Christ, for Every Woman* … and then pass it on to other women and men, so that they will grow in their love for Christ, too.

Matthias Lohmann

Pastor of the Free Evangelical Church Munich, Germany
Chairman, Evangelium21

Jenny Manley has done a great job in this book of making accessible an important topic for every Christian today. This book lifts our gaze to how glorious and majestic Christ is, and it will help you worship Him more. I am grateful for this book and know that it will be a great resource for ladies either on their own or in groups.

Greg Gilbert

Senior Pastor, Third Avenue Baptist Church, Louisville
Author, *Who is Jesus* and *What is the Gospel?*

Jenny Manley shows us the centrality of Christ and His work throughout the whole Scripture. The richness of her work lies in the deep unity she shows between the New and Old Testament in relation to the person and work of Christ. Her work fits well for someone who is newly introduced to the Christian faith, and also for mature Christians who seek solid food for their souls.

Sherif A. Fahim
Professor, Alexandria School of Theology, Alexandria, Egypt
General Director, El-Soora Ministries

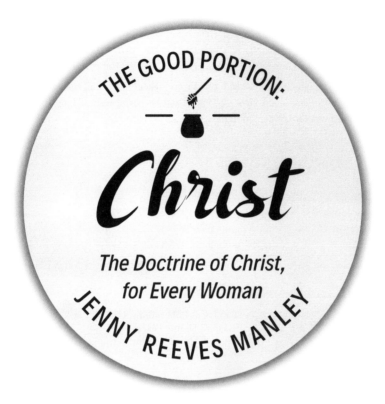

THE GOOD PORTION:

Christ

The Doctrine of Christ,
for Every Woman

JENNY REEVES MANLEY

SERIES EDITOR: KERI FOLMAR

CHRISTIAN
FOCUS

Copyright © Jenny Reeves Manley 2020

paperback ISBN 978-1-5271-0521-8
epub ISBN 978-1-5271-0573-7
mobi ISBN 978-1-5271-0574-4

10 9 8 7 6 5 4 3 2 1

Published in 2020
by
Christian Focus Publications, Ltd.
Geanies House, Fearn,
Ross-shire, IV20 1TW, Scotland.
www.christianfocus.com

Cover design by Pete Barnsley

Printed and bound by
Bell & Bain, Glasgow

CONTENTS

To my husband Josh.
You have taught me about Jesus from His Word,
and you have demonstrated Him with your love.

'My beloved is mine and I am his.' (Song. 2:16)

For my children Reeves, Caroline, Miriam, Harper, and George.
You were both the incentive and the occasional obstacle for this book.
If not for you, I would have finished writing a long time ago,
but if not for you, I never would have started writing at all.

'I pray that out of his glorious riches he may strengthen you with power
through his Spirit in your inner being, so that Christ may dwell in your hearts
through faith. And I pray that you, being rooted and established
in love, may have power, together with all the Lord's holy people, to grasp how
wide and long and high and deep is the love of Christ, and to know this love
that surpasses knowledge — that you may be filled to the measure of all the
fullness of God.' (Eph. 3:16-19, NIV)

Series Preface

The priest pleaded with the young woman to renounce her faith and embrace the Roman Catholic Church. Only sixteen years of age, Lady Jane Grey had been the Protestant Queen of England for nine short days. Her cousin, the staunch Catholic Queen Mary, would pardon her life if only she would recant. Instead, Jane resolutely walked to the scaffold and publicly declared:

> I pray you all, good Christian people, to bear me witness that
> I die a true Christian woman. I do look to be saved by no other
> means, but only by the mercy of God, in the blood of his only
> Son Jesus Christ.[1]

Jane Grey's confidence lay in the sure hope of the resurrection for
those who trust in Christ alone.

Ann Hasseltine struggled to make her decision. She loved
Adoniram and was even drawn by the excitement of exploring
foreign lands. But was she willing to give up all the comforts of
home for the dangers of the unknown? Could she endure leaving
loved ones never to meet them again in this life? Adoniram Judson
was headed to India in 1811 and had asked Ann to join him as
his wife. Never before had any woman left America to become
a missionary to unreached people. Ann's contemplation of Jesus
made the decision for her. In her diary she wrote:

> When I get near to God, and discern the excellence of the
> character of the Lord Jesus, and especially his power and
> willingness to save, I feel desirous, that the whole world should
> become acquainted with this Savior. I am not only willing to
> spend my days among the heathen, in attempting to enlighten
> and save them, but I find much pleasure in the prospect. Yes,
> I am quite willing to give up temporal comforts, and live a life
> of hardship and trial, if it be the will of God.[2]

Mary King stirred her pot as she contemplated Sunday's sermon.
'Cook' was a faithful, godly woman who not only prepared hearty
meals for the boys at Newmarket School, but also served up 'good
strong Calvinistic doctrine' to fifteen-year-old Charles Spurgeon,
who credited her with teaching him his theology:

---

1   Quoted in Faith Cook, *Lady Jane Grey: Nine Day Queen of England* (Darlington:
     Evangelical Press, 2004), p. 198.

2   Quoted in Sharon James, *My Heart in His Hands* (Durham: Evangelical Press,
     1998), p. 38.

Many a time we have gone over the covenant of grace together, and talked of the personal election of the saints, their union to Christ, their final perseverance, and what vital godliness meant; and I do believe that I learnt more from her than I should have learned from any six doctors of divinity of the sort we have nowadays.[3]

Cook dished out spiritual food as well as meat and potatoes, and Charles Spurgeon never forgot what she taught him.

A queen, a bride and a cook: they were all steeped in Christian doctrine – biblical teaching about God. These women didn't just endure theology. They relished the truths of the Christian faith. Doctrine affected their lives and overflowed to impact others.

As women in the modern world we lead busy lives. We may juggle the responsibilities of work and school and home. We wake up in the morning to dirty laundry and an inbox full of email. We go to bed at night after washing dishes, chasing deadlines and rocking babies to sleep. Sometimes life is overwhelming and sometimes it is just mundane. The God who sent His Son into the world to rescue sinners gives meaning to both the overwhelming and the mundane. He created us to enjoy knowing Him, and it is in knowing Him that we find both meaning and joy. Psalm 16:11 says, 'You make known to me the path of life; in your presence there is fullness of joy; at your right hand are pleasures forevermore.' This is why Jesus commended Mary 'who sat at the Lord's feet and listened to his teaching' (Luke 10:39). In the midst of a busy household, Mary was enjoying doctrine – Jesus' teaching about Himself and His Father. She chose 'the good portion' and couldn't tear herself away.

How do you feel about doctrine? Do you dwell on the gospel, meditate on the excellencies of Christ and discuss the doctrines of grace? Do you relish the truths of the Christian faith? This series of books on doctrine for women is an attempt to fuel your enjoyment

---

3   C.H. Spurgeon, *Autobiography: Volume 1 The Early Years* (Edinburgh: Banner of Truth Trust, 1962), p. 39.

of God by encouraging a greater knowledge of Him. It is our hope that the biblical doctrines laid out here will not only increase your head-knowledge but will be driven down into your heart, bearing fruit in your life and overflowing into the lives of others.

Keri Folmar
September 2016

Introduction

No other figure in human history has held the world stage longer than Jesus Christ of Nazareth. No one has been the focus of more attention, whether from devotion or denouncement. No one's life has been scrutinized more carefully or by as many people. No one's words have been memorized or quoted as often as those of Jesus, and certainly no one has been the subject of more books.

So why write another one? Surely nothing can be written that has not already been covered at some point in the past 2,000 years.

I humbly offer two reasons for this book. First, Jesus deserves the worldwide attention He has held. As the most supreme being in the universe, He merits such attention from His creation. He deserves many voices offering analysis, praise, and insight into His identity and His work. Without shame, I offer my own voice to the chorus of those throughout history who have gazed at Jesus and longed to know more. It is my sincere prayer that this book serves many women by providing a Biblically accurate, accessible, and clear picture of Jesus so that we may know Him better and worship Him more.

Second, while many doctrinal books have been written that are a genuine gift to the church and have helped Christians for centuries better understand and follow Christ, those books often have not ended up in the hands of women. I am grateful for the men in my life who have diligently, carefully, and studiously approached Scripture, and have taught it to both men and women. But we should note that Titus 2 demands we women be sound in our doctrine and able to 'teach what is good' to the next generation. Paul clearly presents the pattern of older women teaching younger women, and I long for the women of my generation to grow heartily in theological literacy and then pass it on to the next generation of spiritually strong, joy-filled, theologically-precise women. Matters of doctrine are immeasurably important and practical for women at every stage of life, and this book is intended to be a theological primer for women on the person and work of Christ.

Theology Matters

During the time I was writing this book, I sat with friends whose marriages were crumbling, those whose doubts about God and His goodness lingered as unwanted guests, those who received serious health diagnoses, those who have faced life-threatening persecution, and those who have struggled with seemingly unfair circumstances in life. Some have had wayward and unrepentant children. Some are recovering from trauma or walking through grief. Some have faced serious financial problems. Since I began writing, both my father and my father-in-law have been diagnosed with serious illnesses, and my mother and 'mother-in-love' have been unexpectedly handed the role of caregiver. In all of these difficult situations with my friends and family, their doctrine of Christ has shaped the way they approach suffering in this life. In fact, one's Christology may be the single most important factor in determining how we approach the various trials of life.

In addition to aiding in our trials, our theology also affects our worship of the Lord Jesus. Several times as I was writing this book and was reading and thinking about the theological truths covered in it, I had to stop what I was doing and simply praise God for who He is and what He has accomplished for us through Christ – sometimes to the detriment of the time I had set aside to write. One day I was writing at a local coffee shop and was deeply moved by a fresh understanding of the truth that the Son of God left the glories of heaven to humbly become a man in order to rescue us from our hopeless state of rebellion against Him. I could do nothing else but stop and praise God for who He is and what He has done. Oblivious patrons continued their whispered gossip and muted laughter, totally unaware of my private worship service as I closed my computer and prayed to God, longing only to hear the voices of men and angels singing praise to the Lord. It should not surprise us that the study of doctrine produces worship – even if it does tend to slow down the writing process a bit. God instructs us to worship Him 'in spirit and in truth' (John 4:23). We worship God by the power of the Holy Spirit in truth, namely the Truth revealed to us in the Bible as the person of Christ.

Our natural response to growth in theological understanding of who Jesus is and what He did for us will be greater delight and more earnest praise. That was certainly true of Paul. In the first 11 chapters of Romans he carefully lays out the good news that the righteousness of Christ is available to us through faith. After a rich and lengthy meditation on the gospel, he bursts into glorious praise: 'Oh, the depth of the riches and wisdom and knowledge of God! How unsearchable are his judgments and how inscrutable his ways!'

Even before he applies the truth of the gospel, he sings out in worship to God. When we sing the Romans Doxology today, we are singing Paul's words of praise in response to the theological truth he had spent pages meditating on. True knowledge of the Lord produces joy-filled worship in His blood-bought children. May our worship of Jesus motivate and equip us to confidently tell the world about Him with clarity and truth.

The Road Ahead

This book is arranged in two parts – who Jesus is and what He has accomplished. First, as we look at who He is, we consider Him as the main character in the storyline of Scripture. Without this foundation in place, it is difficult to understand the role He plays in human history and more importantly, redemptive history. We then consider the two natures of Jesus, each in turn. We consider how we can be certain that Jesus is the divine Son of God, and then we meditate on that truth. Next, we look closely at what we know about His humanity and again, reflect on it. We could have considered these aspects of Jesus' life in reverse order, but we'll start with His divinity because that's who He was from eternity past. Jesus always has been and always will be divine. His humanity was added to His divinity. The first section concludes with our considering just that – how one man can be both fully human and fully divine at the same time. I do not attempt to answer every question that may arise in considering such a difficult topic. But where Scripture is clear, I attempt to be clear as well.

The second section of the book focuses on what Jesus accomplished. We look at God's detailed rescue plan to save sinners from His wrath and how Jesus perfectly fulfilled the plan. Then we will consider more specifically the atonement, narrowing in on how penal substitution is the most accurate view of the atoning work of Christ. We conclude with a brief introduction and reflection on the unique privilege of the believer being united to Christ.

It is important to note from the beginning that I take the position and write from the assumption that the Bible is true. I believe the Bible to be without error, inspired by the Holy Spirit, and preserved today in its intended form. Many resources exist that delve deeper into these issues and explain the basis of why I take this position. One good resource is the book in this series *The Good Portion: The Doctrine of Scripture for Every Woman* by Keri Folmar. She addresses many issues about Scripture's inerrancy and purpose.

In the paraphrased words of Martin Luther, I am just one beggar showing another beggar where to find bread. If you do not yet know Jesus in the personal way described in this book, my prayer is that you will realize your hunger and be fed by the Bread of Life, the only one who is eternally satisfying. If you already know Jesus, I pray your soul will be nourished as He is held high in these pages. I hope that you find true delight in studying His life, death, and resurrection. And whether you have known the Lord Jesus for decades of your life or you are just a curious inquirer, I pray the words here will stir your soul and point you to the One for whom your soul was made. As you read the following pages, may you worship the true King and may your love for Him abound more and more (Phil. 1:9). I hope this book is one pebble on your long pathway of knowing and worshiping Jesus eternally.

Part One
The Person of Christ

Chapter 1

Who is Jesus?

Sarah grew up in a Christian home and attended church throughout her childhood. She listened attentively in Sunday School as the teacher taught stories from the Bible, but as an adult she has struggled to find any relevance in the Bible. Most of the stories from her elementary understanding of scripture seem strange to her as an adult. A boy fighting a giant with just a few rocks? A boat full of animals saved from a flood? A sea separated into dry land? Are these stories just children's fables? What do they have to do with God? Even more directly, Sarah wants to know what they have to do with her.

We love a good story, especially a narrative of good fighting evil or love being pursued at all costs. Long lasting are those epic tales of beauty being concealed until just the right moment or the unlikely lovers overcoming odds and obstacles to find each other. From childhood, we want to hear these stories told over and over. Even when we know the outcome, we want to watch and re-watch them depicted on the screen or the stage. Perhaps we find such pleasure in these tales because our lives are playing out in one.

Hold that thought...

To tell us what He is like, God did not simply drop a book down from heaven. He could have. Some religions believe their god revealed truth about himself in a vision or visions to one person who wrote it down in a sacred book. Mormons and Muslims believe this. In other religions, the sacred text consists mainly of a catalog of approved behaviors, rituals, or customs. Sects of Hinduism, Buddhism, and Sikhism follow their sacred writings. But only Christians believe God deliberately revealed Himself over time in a story. The story certainly includes rituals, ceremonies, and laws, but like a great symphony each of those are only parts of the whole. The parts cannot be rightly understood and appreciated without hearing the full symphony, just as the symphony is not as beautiful when any of the parts are missing.

Because God chose to carefully reveal Himself over time through a sweeping and dramatic story, we learn more than mere facts about Him; we see His character in action as He binds Himself over generations to a people and teaches them about Himself.

The drama unfolds as a love story, with the surprising and good news that God gets glory through His gracious and steadfast pursuit of a most unlikely object of His affection – the often unlovely and consistently rebellious people He created. The fullness of God's character comes into view at the entrance of His Son, whom Scripture describes as the image of the invisible Father (Col. 1:15; John 1:18). The Son turns out to be the main character of the story as He gives Himself sacrificially for His beloved bride.

While the Scriptures are made up of hundreds of stories that are often told on their own, they are merely parts of this grander tale. They are like scenes of a play – occasionally humorous, sometimes tragic, and often so full of darkness and despair we see only glimpses of hope that things won't always be as they appear. The real value in knowing the storyline of the Bible though is found in what it teaches us about the main characters.

Act I: A Redeemer Promised

The story opens at the very good beginning with God as creator of all things – the day and night; the sun, moon, and stars; and the animals on land, sea, and air. The first week spectacularly climaxed with the creation of the first people being made 'in the image of God' (Gen. 1:27). God generously and graciously placed Adam and Eve in a perfect garden where He communed directly with them, and they had unfiltered access to Him. He gave them to each other for their companionship, enjoyment, and so they could multiply and fill the earth with offspring. He provided them an abundance of good food to eat and easy access to it all. He gave them good work to do and a beautiful and luxurious office space to do it in. He loved His people, and out of this lavish love and generosity He gave them the unique privilege and unparalleled responsibility of tending to His creation. They alone had the opportunity to image their Maker in the way they cared for God's creation on His behalf. Talk about living your best life!

But instead of living in obedience to this good God and under His obviously good authority and blessing, Adam and Eve turned against Him. They should have contentedly ruled over creation, but instead they listened to the crafty lies of the serpent, letting God's enemy rule over them. In eating the forbidden fruit, they forfeited all the rights and privileges of the good life they had in Eden and formed a massive chasm between themselves and their God. Oh, and important to the story is that they did so on behalf of all of us. They were representatives of Humanity – for everyone in the entire world for all time.

FIRST PROMISED IN THE GARDEN

The world was irrevocably altered after this fall of mankind into sin. The very good world of Eden found in Genesis 1-2 suddenly became the sin-cursed, thorn-infected world of Genesis 3. Adam and Eve's rebellion against God was far more than a mere mistake; it introduced evil into the perfect world God had created. The serpent had promised the eyes of Adam and Eve would be opened if they rebelled against God, but what they saw was shame. After their transgression, the previously innocent world was filled with guilt as the first couple became aware of their nakedness and covered themselves with fig leaves. Their attempt to cover their own shame left them hiding from their God. Their physical nakedness pointed toward their spiritual helplessness as they stood in obvious need of covering.

The consequences of this first sin were catastrophic. God declared that the fruitfulness He had so generously given to Adam and Eve would now come only with great difficulty. For Eve, being fruitful and multiplying would be marked by great pain from that point forward. For Adam, His previously fruitful bounty would now come through difficult toil, thorns, and thistles (Gen. 3:16-19). As a result of sin, Adam and Eve's lives were marked by pain and distance from their God. If man were ever to know a garden-like state and unity with God again, God Himself would have to bring it about. Remarkably, that is what God promised the man and the woman right after the fall as He moved in a surprisingly gracious way.

Instead of striking them dead immediately for their rebellion, God promised His people that through the pain of childbearing He would provide a Savior for mankind. Judgment was coming, but God would provide a path for salvation through it. God cursed the serpent and told of enmity between him and Eve's offspring, with the promised offspring ultimately prevailing. 'He will crush your head, and you will strike his heel' (Gen. 3:15 NIV). Despite Adam and Eve's act of cosmic treason, God graciously killed an animal and made 'garments of skins and clothed them' (Gen. 3:21). This foreshadowed One who would come to cover His people's spiritual nakedness – a serpent-crushing Savior who would cover His people not simply with garments of animal skin but robes of righteousness, purchased with blood.

Even though the first people were blessed and declared 'very good' (Gen. 1:31) by God at creation, just six chapters into the story, we read of mankind's spiral into wickedness. Adam and Eve's rebellion toward God had grown into a full-blown mutiny of mankind against the Creator. 'The Lord saw that the wickedness of man was great in the earth, and that every intention of the thoughts of his heart was only evil continually.' What was God's response to His creation choosing such evil? 'The Lord regretted that he had made man on the earth, and it grieved him to his heart' (Gen. 6:5-7). God's wrath against the sinful human race was so great that He destroyed almost every living thing on the earth through a worldwide flood. God spared only the blessed passengers who took refuge in Noah's ark. This story is not a child's fable, but rather an early (and graphic) scene that highlights God's wrath towards those in rebellion against Him. And yet in it, we also see another beautiful picture of God's grace. Again we see that through judgment, God provided a path of salvation for some. He provided a way for His beloved people (Noah and his family) to come safely through those treacherous flood waters.

But not even catastrophic annihilation of life destroyed the wickedness in men's hearts. We do not even have to turn a page in the Bible before we see it in Noah himself. Even though he had just been the most favored and blessed man on the planet, Noah promptly came out of the ark – and sinned again. Much like his first parents, Noah took the fruit of the land and turned it against his Creator (Gen. 9:20-21). In the flood, God removed people from the earth because of their sin, but He did not remove sin from the people of the earth.

THE LAMB WHO WAS SLAIN

God revealed increasingly more about Himself and the coming serpent-crushing Offspring during the following centuries of history recorded in the Bible. In one scene, God called Abram (later renamed Abraham) out of idol worship to be a follower of the one, true God. God vowed to make him the father of many nations, giving him as many descendants as there were stars in the night sky, and promising that in Abraham the entire earth would be blessed. But instead of a tent full of children, silent and lonely decades of his wife's barrenness followed – until God finally provided Abraham and Sarah a promised son they named Isaac. But incomprehensibly, God told Abraham to sacrifice his beloved son Isaac on Mount Moriah. Right as Abraham – filled with trust in his God – obediently reached out his hand to grab the knife that would slay his beloved son, God intervened and provided a ram as a substitute in Isaac's place (Gen. 22:1-14). This innocent animal gave another hint about the character of God and the coming Offspring. Because of God's great love for mankind, He would provide the necessary sacrifice to satisfy His anger toward sin.

Hundreds of years later the promised descendants of Abraham found themselves in distress. They were not demonstrating their favored-status or being a blessing to the world; they had instead become slaves in Egypt, outsiders in a foreign land, who had no freedom, favor, or might. During God's dramatic liberation of His people from this helpless situation, He revealed additional details about both His character and the coming rescuer. On the night before Moses led the Israelite people out of slavery in Egypt, God instructed His people to slaughter a spotless lamb and put the blood of the animal on their doorposts. For every household that was not covered by the blood of the lamb, the firstborn son would be killed by the angel of death. For every household covered by the blood of the lamb, the angel of death would pass over, allowing life instead of death, providing salvation for His people in the midst of

His judgment (Exod. 12). In this scene, we meet the God whose holiness and love require justice, yet He offers grace. Both justice and grace are provided for through the blood of a sacrificed lamb. The Israelites responded obediently, and they and their children were rescued out of slavery. But they could not have known then that the Passover lamb pointed to another – 'the Lamb of God who takes away the sin of the world!' (1 John 1:29).

THE SUFFERING SERVANT

This lamb was described by the prophet Isaiah, who pronounced judgment on the Jewish people of his day for their failure to keep covenant with God. But Isaiah also spoke hopefully of God's future work to redeem His people and renew the entire world through the coming Offspring, who He said would suffer for them. 'But he was pierced for our transgressions; he was crushed for our iniquities; upon him was the chastisement that brought us peace, and with his wounds we are healed' (Isa. 53:5). Through this suffering servant, God's people would be blessed – but only through his wounds. The serpent-crusher would himself be crushed for His people's inequities.

A LIFE FORETOLD

Act I includes other prophets divinely revealing facts about the birth, life, and death of the coming Offspring. Isaiah refers to a child who will be born of a virgin whose name, Immanuel, means 'God with us' (Isa. 7:14). Micah predicts a ruler over Israel who is from the ancient of days who will be born in the town of Bethlehem (Micah 5:2). Zechariah prophesied that Jerusalem would one day praise the redeemer who would provide salvation to Israel, and he specifically foretold that this divinely appointed one would ride into Jerusalem on a donkey (Zech. 9:9). The Old Testament ends with God's people still looking for this Offspring – a lamb of God, a suffering servant, a cover for the people's sin, one who would crush the head of the serpent.

Act II: The Redeemer's Great Rescue

The curtains open in Act II (the New Testament) with an unveiling of the news that the long-promised, long-anticipated Offspring has finally come in the flesh. Unexpected plot twists escalate the dramatic entrance of this baby into the world. We find out the mother of the promised One is curiously a virgin. She has no place to deliver this Lamb of God and as it ends up, his first bed was a feeding trough. A king tries to have the baby killed after a mysterious light in the sky attracts the attention of scholars from foreign lands. His family has to flee in the night to a neighboring country to protect his young life. But perhaps most surprising of all – although it was masterfully foreshadowed – is that this baby who has come to rescue the world turns out to be God Himself.

In Jesus the shadows disperse into full light. The One sent by God to rescue His people is none other than God Himself. God sent His own Son to become man, in every way just like His people, yet still fully God. Unlike all other men throughout history, Jesus lived a life without sin. He resisted the temptation to join the people's wicked rebellion, and instead provided the way to eternal life. He did so in another shocking plot twist. Instead of demanding political power and earthly glory, He personally took the punishment the rebels deserve by dying a painful and shameful death on a cross. The suffering servant prophesied by Isaiah took on Himself God's rightful and righteous wrath toward sin, bearing the crushing weight of God's punishment for all His people's sin. However, in perhaps the last and most dramatic plot twist of all, He did not stay dead. In a glorious and climactic scene, after three days in the grave – just as was prophesied (Hosea 6:1-3; Matt. 16:21; John 2:19; 1 Cor. 15:4) – Jesus rose from the dead. Following His resurrection, He appeared to hundreds of people, commissioned

His disciples to proclaim His kingdom everywhere, and ascended into heaven, where He reigns over all the universe. He is there even now, ruling over the world.

Tragically, those people who never put down their sword of rebellion against God will face His full judgment and the punishment they deserve, an eternity in hell. But remarkably, through this judgment God provided a way of salvation through Jesus. One day He will return to earth and gather all of His people, living and dead. These people, former rebels who have surrendered to Jesus through repentance and faith in Him will stand confidently before God covered in the righteousness and forgiveness of their rescuer, the Lamb of God, the Savior Jesus Christ. He will then usher in a new heaven and a new earth, where God will live and reign with His people forever. In Act II we find out Jesus did not just come to rescue His people, but in His great love, He takes them as His own. So close is Christ's relationship with these former rebels, Scripture calls them 'beloved' (Col. 3:12) and 'in Christ'.

The New Testament explains the life, death, and resurrection of Jesus. It records the birth of the church, Christ's bride (Eph. 5:24-27, 2 Cor. 11:2, Rev. 19:7-9, 21:1-2), and gives instruction for God's people on how to live while we wait for His eventual return to earth. The New Testament provides hope for God's people in knowing that one day Christ will gather us together and a new era will begin as the original story began – God's people in perfect communion with Him in the perfect place He will create, full of His abundant generosity and love. Former rebels who have been rescued from their helpless distress and covered with the blood of the lamb will live once again with their God. This happily-ever-after love story never ends, as Christ's bride lives with Him in perfect joy for all eternity. Unlike Eden, this time sin will never enter the story again.

That is the story of the Bible from Genesis to Revelation. The 66 books of the Bible, while written over thousands of years on different continents and by dozens of different authors, tell of this singular drama of man's great rebellion against God. It tells us of the judgment coming for sinful men and women, but it also holds out for us a gracious and merciful redeemer named Jesus sent to rescue God's people to reconcile them with God.

Audience or Actors?

One of my favorite stories is *Les Misérables*, the powerful tale that takes place in an embroiled nineteenth-century Paris, in which one gracious act weaves together the lives of an undeserving prisoner, an over-zealous policeman, and a destitute prostitute. I have read the book. I have seen the musical performed in multiple countries, have watched the movie dozens of times, and listened to the soundtrack hundreds (maybe thousands!) of times. The music and the story never grow old to me. The creativity of the love story, the themes of redemption, and the contrast depicted between bondage to the law and the freedom of grace captivate me. But I enjoy the tale merely from the audience as a passive observer.

The story unfolding throughout human history with Jesus as the main character is not one we enjoy as spectators. Jesus is *our* great Rescuer. He has come to save *us* from our rebellion against God. And as we study the life of this man who came into the world to rescue His bride from peril, we find ourselves not merely passively observing a story on stage. We find our personal stories inside this bigger one. Our lives are taking part in this drama as we play the part of the rebellious crowd trying to overthrow the benevolent King. We are the objects of His love and the reason God had to come to earth to pursue His beloved. We are the often unlovely and consistently rebellious people that God has rescued through Jesus.

In this story found in the Bible, we are presented in truth as hopeless and helpless without a redeemer. We need a rescuer. Jesus comes on stage in Act II and is shown to be the promised One who has finally come to rescue His beloved bride, and as such He deserves our praise, complete devotion, and allegiance for all eternity.

QUESTIONS

WHO IS JESUS?

The story of the Bible is the love story of a holy God in pursuit of His wayward people. After the Garden of Eden, generations of God's people remain separated from their Creator, and yet the Old Testament is full of God's promises that one will come to rescue them. As God gives His people pictures and promises of this would-be hero, we see a progressive unveiling of who God is. The main character of the story is the hero: Jesus, the God-man, and He takes the punishment the people deserve for their sin, securing their happily ever after with Him.

1. What does the overarching story of scripture have to do with Sarah (p. 21)?

2. The main character in the story of scripture is Jesus. Who are the other main characters? What role do you play in this drama? The bride of Christ is made up of those people who have turned away from their sins and trusted in Jesus. Have you?

3. God could have told us all we needed to know about Him at one time. But instead the Bible was written over centuries by many authors from several different cultures. In other words, God slowly unveiled Himself to His people over time. Why was God's revelation of His character in this way helpful to our understanding who He is?

4. Genesis 3:15 provides our first glimpse that God will send a rescuer for His people. In what ways does this passage foretell of the work that must be done by Jesus?

5. From the very beginning of the narrative, God makes promises to His people. What does this tell us about God and what does it tell us about the Scriptures?

6. In all narratives, there is a problem that needs solving. What is the conflict that needs to be addressed in the narrative found in Scripture from Genesis to Revelation? Read these passages for reference: Genesis 6:5-7, Exodus 16:2-3, Judges 21:25, Amos 5:12-13.

7. The New Testament uses several analogies besides that of a bride to describe those Jesus came to rescue. Which ones can you think of? Here are a few references to get you thinking: Ephesians 2:19-22, 1 Corinthians 3:16-17, 1 Corinthians 12:12.

8. In your own words in 2-4 sentences, write the storyline of the Bible, starting with the creation of all things.

Chapter 2

Fully God

Sophia is a friend of yours who occasionally attends your church. Recently Sophia met a Muslim neighbor and the two women are quickly becoming good friends. Last week over coffee Myriam shared with Sophia that Islam teaches that there is one God and that Jesus was only a prophet. Myriam explained that she believed God had sent several prophets to tell the world about Him — Abraham, Moses, and Noah were all prophets from God, as was Jesus. Sophia has begun asking questions and wants to know if Jesus really is God. She has come to you asking what difference it would make for her to believe in the divinity of Jesus. What do you tell her?

Who is Jesus? That is the most important question any of us will ever answer. It captivated the Jewish community over 2,000 years ago as a man claiming to be God entered the stage of human history. Generations of people across civilizations have been wrestling with the same question ever since.

The answer you will get to that question varies widely depending on who is answering it. Was He merely a good man? A moral teacher? A revolutionary? Or was He the very Son of God?

Widely accepted historical evidence points to an actual person named Jesus who was born between 3 and 6 B.C. in Bethlehem. He worked as a carpenter, lived into His 30s, and died at the hands of the Jewish authorities on a Roman cross outside of Jerusalem. Even secular historians agree that He had a following of disciples and that many men and women in His day believed that He rose from the dead. Beyond these generally accepted conclusions, however, people differ greatly in their opinions of who He was, who He claimed to be, and what His significance is today.

A few years after Jesus' death and resurrection, the Jewish religious elite grew weary of and even hostile toward Jesus' followers who continued to insist that He was the promised Savior who had risen from the dead. One day the Jewish Council was considering the fate of Jesus' apostles and the destruction of this new sect when a Pharisee named Gamaliel spoke words of caution, perhaps wiser than he even realized. He said, '...if this plan or this undertaking is of man, it will fail; but if it is of God, you will not be able to overthrow them. You might even be found opposing God!' (Acts 5:38-39) The council let the apostles go free that day with only a beating, in hopes that the revolution that had started would quietly go away. Instead, it grew. And now 2,000 years later, Jesus is followed by more people than ever before in world history.

One explanation skeptics offer to explain Jesus' lingering popularity is to portray Him as merely a popular moral teacher of His day. They concede that He was a good man, but they stop there. The prominent modern atheist Richard Dawkins recently tweeted, 'Paradoxically, Jesus's reputation suffers from his being deified. As a moral teacher he is admirable but overshadowed by silly worship.'[1] Dawkins and others argue Jesus could be admired in the same way

---

1   https://twitter.com/richarddawkins/status/677901749190074368

Gandhi is for attributes such as His strong leadership abilities and His moral teachings, but anyone who believes Jesus is God (or worships Him as such) is labeled foolish.

Those who might describe themselves as 'spiritual' but do not necessarily subscribe to any one particular religion often view Jesus as *a* path but not necessarily *the* path to God. They feel no particular disdain for Jesus, and in fact may even celebrate that their Christian friends found something that 'works' for them. However, this group rejects the exclusive claims of Jesus, arguing His is merely one way up a heavily-trod mountain where everyone eventually reaches the top. Sincerity of faith, not the object of one's faith, is their test.

Another prominent theory is that Jesus was more than a common man, but less than God. Usually, those who argue this position think that Jesus was sent on a mission from God. He lived a remarkable life and did and said good things; however, being sent from God is not equal to being God. They conclude that Jesus' followers were overcome by their zeal and exaggerated who He claimed to be, like an embellished obituary.

This explanation of Jesus' popularity is prevalent in the Middle East, where I live. Muslims believe that Jesus should be honored as one of God's prophets but calling Jesus God is blasphemy. They believe that in the years after Jesus' death, His followers recorded facts about His life and teaching, but that over the centuries the Bible was changed. Original copies were lost, and translations through the centuries changed the meaning and claims of the text. They argue that today's Bible contains so many errors it can no longer be trusted and that the real Jesus should not be worshiped. Islam teaches God sent a final prophet, Muhammed, to correct the mistakes made by those who zealously followed Jesus.

If we Christians are honest, it is audacious to believe the claim that a crucified man who lived thousands of years ago was actually God who had come to earth as a human. Without divine revelation of the truth of who Jesus is, we can easily understand how one would call this belief an embellishment of the truth, or even 'silly.' When comprehensively surveying the evidence found in Scripture, however, we can have confidence that before Jesus was from Nazareth, He was the Son of God from heaven. The roll call of those who testify to His divine Sonship is long and authoritative.

There is a popular saying that if something looks like a duck and talks like a duck and walks like a duck, it is a duck. In this same way, we can know the man Jesus is God. Consider these aspects of His life that show He was uniquely God: He was prophesied from ancient times to be God, acted like God, was called by the holy names of God, and will be worshiped for all eternity for being God. If He looks like God, talks like God, and acts like God, we can be certain Jesus truly is God.

God Himself is Coming!

Ever since the Garden of Eden when God promised a seed of the woman would one day come to defeat her enemy, God's people held onto the hope that the anointed serpent crusher was coming to rescue them. A chorus of prophetic voices thousands of years strong gave hope to the wayward people of God to press on. No single stanza gave the full picture of who Jesus would be, but many beautiful notes along the way pointed directly to the spiritual nature of this anointed One.

ISAIAH

The prophet Isaiah beautifully sang one of these choruses hundreds of years before Jesus was born. Right after breaking the bad news to the Israelites that their persistent sin would lead to a future captivity, Isaiah comforted them by reminding them of the promised Offspring. He described the long sought-after Savior in this way:

> For to us a child is born, to us a son is given;
> and the government shall be upon his shoulder, and his name
> shall be called

> Wonderful Counselor, Mighty God,
> Everlasting Father, Prince of Peace (Isa 9:6).

Prophets don't casually throw around nicknames like 'Mighty God' and 'Everlasting Father.' The language he is using to describe the Savior is unmistakably divine.

Isaiah prophesied the divinity of the coming Savior a second time when he told the Israelites how they would be able to identify him. He said that there would be a man in the wilderness who had a unique role as messenger, and his job would be to announce that the promised serpent-crusher had finally come. In describing this courier of good news, Isaiah wrote: 'A voice cries: In the wilderness prepare the way of the LORD; make straight in the desert a highway for our *God*' (Isa. 40:3, emphasis mine). The messenger would prepare the way for *the LORD, our God*. The prophet Malachi also prophesied that this messenger would prepare the way for *the LORD's* arrival (Mal. 3:1). This language was unmistakable: God Himself was coming!

JOHN THE BAPTIST

Logically then, each of the Gospels begins with an introduction to this messenger, John the Baptist. He is not to be confused with John the Apostle, the beloved disciple who wrote the Gospel of John; rather, John the Baptist was the messenger sent by God to proclaim the inauguration of God's great rescue plan. Mark uses both the passage from Isaiah and the passage from Malachi to announce John's arrival (Mark 1:2-3). John was 'baptizing in the wilderness and proclaiming a baptism of repentance for the forgiveness of sins' (Mark 1:4) to make straight a highway for God. When he made the announcement that God's people had been anticipating for so long, he broke a 400-year prophetic silence like a loud cymbal crash that was a glorious wake-up call.

One day John saw Jesus coming toward him for baptism. Recognizing the One who was before him, John said, 'Behold, the Lamb of God, who takes away the sin of the world!' (John 1:29).

After his encounter with Jesus, he boldly proclaimed, 'I have seen and have borne witness that this is the Son of God' (John 1:34). John the Baptist, whose purpose was to announce the arrival of the promised anointed One, told the Israelites that the rescuer they had been waiting for had arrived. The Savior had finally come – and the Savior was none other than God Himself!

TO FULFILL THEM

With this public decree by the prophetic messenger, the public ministry of Jesus began. He wasted no time in claiming to be the Messiah (meaning 'anointed one'), the long-promised offspring of Eve who would crush the head of the serpent. The Jewish people who had been waiting for centuries for this Savior were expecting a king, a descendant from David who would rule over their nation bringing about political power and defeating Israel's enemies.

So the claim made by Jesus in His first recorded message – the famous Sermon on the Mount – would have been stunning to the Galilean audience. He boldly stated that He was the point of all the sacred Old Testament writings. 'Do not think I have come to abolish the Law or the Prophets; I have not come to abolish them *but to fulfill them*' (Matt. 5:17, emphasis mine). Shock waves must have rippled through the Jewish audience as they heard Jesus declare Himself to be the end goal of Scripture. As He explained to them that Scripture's prophetic purposes were fulfilled in Him, He told them that they were looking at the promised One for whom they had been waiting. Stephen Wellum wrote, 'Implied though it may be, the Christological claim here is simply staggering. Jesus understood Himself to be the eschatological goal of the entire Old Testament and the sole authoritative interpreter of its teaching. In other words, Jesus self-identified as a man who shared authority with God, the author of the Law under His covenant with Israel.'[2]

---

2   Stephen J. Wellum, *Christ Alone: The Uniqueness of Jesus as Savior* (Grand Rapids, MI: Zondervan, 2017), p. 62.

Their wait was over. The serpent-crushing rescuer had arrived. That day Jesus explained His life would be a fulfilment of all the Old Testament laws and prophesies about the Messiah.

At the end of His earthly ministry, Jesus was able to look back on His life and clearly explain how He did this. The recently-resurrection Jesus traveled from Jerusalem to Emmaus with two people who did not recognize Him. Jesus listened as the couple discussed the headline events during the Passover week. They must have been baffled at this stranger who seemed to know nothing of the breaking news that had shaken Jerusalem, and so they recounted the unexpected crucifixion of the popular teacher and the reports that His body was now missing from His tomb. Jesus knew they did not understand the promises and pictures about the Messiah from the Old Testament, and He asked them, 'Was it not necessary that the Christ should suffer these things and enter into his glory?' He then used the opportunity to explain how all of the Scriptures beginning with Moses and the prophets were fulfilled in Him (see Luke 24:13-35).

Before Jesus ascended to heaven, He wanted His disciples to be confident in their understanding of His life. He told them 'that everything written about me in the Law of Moses and the Prophets and the Psalms must be fulfilled' and He opened their minds 'to understand the Scriptures, and said to them, "Thus it is written, that the Christ should suffer and on the third day rise from the dead, and that repentance and forgiveness of sins should be proclaimed in his name to all nations"' (Luke 24:44-47).

Jesus perfectly fulfilled Scripture's prophecies about the divine nature of the Messiah. Jesus, Mighty God, had come to save His people.

God's Character Displayed in Him

God, because He is God, has certain unique privileges and powers that no other being possesses. Man reflects the image of God but does not possess God's divine attributes. Think of the sun and the moon. The moon reflects the light from the sun, but it does not have the make-up of gases and intense heat that defines the sun. It displays some of the properties of the sun (like providing light), but it only reflects the sun's light. It is not made up of hot plasma nor does it create a gravitational field around it strong enough to hold a solar system in place. Likewise, we reflect the image of our Creator, but we are mere men and women, not the one, true, holy God. God possesses attributes unique to Himself. For example, only God is eternal. Only God has all power and knows all things. By definition, these attributes belong solely to God; His creatures do not possess any of them.

Yet, time and again in the Bible, Jesus demonstrates more than a *reflection* of God's character. He exhibits a *possession* of His attributes. He is described as being omnipotent, omnipresent, and omniscient. He is shown to be Creator of all, one who could forgive sins, and the judge of all men. In other words, He *acted* like God, both eternally and during His time on earth.

OMNIPOTENT

Yahweh is a powerful God in the Old Testament. Right from the beginning, He majestically showcased His omnipotence when He spoke all things into existence out of nothing. He made other gods look like the worthless idols they were. Think about dismembered Dagon lying face down before the ark of the Lord (1 Sam. 5:4). Or the Baal worshipers, dripping in their own blood, pleading with their god to send fire. But 'No one answered; no one paid attention' (1 King 18:25) while the all-consuming fire of Yahweh mocked their disbelief. God is praised in the Psalms for being so powerful that His enemies cannot stand against Him (Ps. 66), and even the stricken Job confessed God's purposes cannot be thwarted because God can do all things (Job 42:2). God rhetorically asked Jeremiah, 'Is anything too hard for me?' (Jer. 32:27). He asked Sarah the same question as the barren 89-year-old laughed at God's promise of motherhood (Gen. 18:14).

Jesus displayed this same power that God paraded through the Old Testament. Throughout His ministry, Jesus repeatedly showed He had power over people, nature, sickness, demons, and death. When He called His disciples, they immediately left everything to follow Him. When He instructed the wind and the waves to be silent, they obeyed (Matt. 8:23-27; Mark 4:36-41; Luke 8:22-25). When He wanted the water to become a walking path, it complied (Matt. 14:22-33; Mark 6:45-51; John 6:16-21); and when He wanted it to be wine, the atomic structure of the liquid obeyed His command instantly and six jars of water became the most famous barrels of wine in history (John 2:1-11). When He commanded the sick to be well, they were instantly healed (Matt. 9:35; Luke 17:12-16; John 9:6-7); when He told demons to depart, they left (Matt. 17:18; Mark 9:25-27; Mark 1:34;). When He ordered dead people to rise, they breathed with new life – and one even walked out of a grave he had been in for four days (John 11:1-44; Luke 7:11-17). Jesus demonstrated His authority over all creation, and all of creation obeyed His word. Paul wrote about Jesus' subjection of all things to Himself (Phil. 3:21), and Jesus' divinity was on display for all those who encountered Him or heard of Him as both His actions and His words testified that He is God.

Only God has that kind of authority and power, and Jesus wielded it on earth.

Omnipresent

Unlike humans who occupy a finite space and time, God's presence is everywhere at the same time. God told the prophet Jeremiah that He fills both the heavens and the earth, so man cannot hide Himself from God in secret places. God is everywhere and sees everything (Jer. 23:23-24). Clearly, this attribute belongs only to God and not finite people bound by the laws of nature. Yet, Jesus promises to be with and among His gathered church (Matt. 18:20), and assured Paul He was with him decades after the ascension (Acts 18:10). He even promises to be with His people until the end of all time (Matt. 28:18). Only God is omnipresent, and Jesus is with us wherever we are.

OMNISCIENT

In the Old Testament the Lord God was praised for knowing all things. Isaiah declared it (Isa. 55:8-9). Job accepted it (Job 37:16). The psalmists sang out in praise because of it (Ps. 139 and others). In the New Testament, we read 'he knows everything' (1 John 3:20). He knows big things like our secret sins (Ps. 69:5) and who His elect are (Rom. 8:29). And He knows small details like when a single sparrow falls to the ground and the exact number of hairs on each of our heads (Matt. 10:29-30).

Jesus demonstrated a unique ability to know things mere mortals cannot know. He knew the private thoughts of the men and women around Him (Luke 5:22, 11:17, Matt. 9:4, Matt. 12:25). He spoke with specificity about the details of the life of the Samarian woman, whom He had never met (John 4:29). Early into His ministry He knew His disciple Judas Iscariot would betray Him (John 6:70-71). He knew Nathaniel had been sitting under a fig tree when his brother told him of Jesus (John 1:48). He instructed His disciples where to go to find a donkey and colt tied up that had never been ridden before (Matt. 21:1-6) and how to find a man who had a room they would use for the last supper (Luke 22:7-13, Matt. 26:17-19). He knew Peter would deny Him on the night of His arrest and even how many times He would do so (Matt. 26:33-35, Mark 14:29-31, Luke 22:33-34, John 13:36-38).

Jesus even foretold His own suffering, death, and resurrection (Matt. 16:21). In fact, three different times He told His disciples as plainly as He could that He would suffer and die, but that He would rise again on the third day. 'He then began to teach them the Son of Man must suffer many things and be rejected by the elders, the chief priests and the teachers of the law, and that he must be killed and after three days rise again.' (Mark 8:31-32, NIV). Sometime later He said about himself, 'They will kill him, and after three days he will rise' (Mark 9:31, NIV). A third time He tells them, '[the chief priests and teachers] will condemn him to death and will hand him over the Gentiles, who will mock him and spit on him, flog him and kill him. Three days later he will rise' (Mark 10:33-4, NIV). Only the omniscient God knows the future, and Jesus holds the future in His hands.

You may recall the instance where Jesus specifically said He did *not* know about His second coming. He told His disciples no one knows the date and time He would return to a final judgment of the world – only the Father knew that information (Matt. 24:36, Mark 13:32). How does the One who is tasked with judging the world not know when that divine appointment will be? As part of the Trinity, the Son of God knows all things that the Father and the Spirit know. They have one singular mind and will. But when the Son of Man took on humanity, He voluntarily took on a human mind with limited knowledge as a man. He cooperated with the normal limitations of humanity, one of which was possessing a mind with knowledge that changes over time. We know this is true of Jesus because Luke told us He 'increased in wisdom' (Luke 2:52). In a later chapter on how Jesus could be both fully divine and fully man at the same time we explore this mysterious idea further. But for now, we see Jesus spoke truthfully that in that moment He did not know the time of His second coming. Of course, that does not mean He still does not know. After His resurrection, Peter says to Him, 'You know all things' (John 21:17), and Jesus does not correct or rebuff him. At that point He was the resurrected Son of God, the One who would represent His people in heaven, done with His work on earth. Post-resurrected King Jesus does not need knowledge revealed to Him from the Father through the Spirit. He possesses all the knowledge of the Father and the Spirit.

FORGIVING SINS

Just this morning as I was making coffee for myself and breakfast for my children, I spoke in an unnecessarily harsh tone with my husband Josh. He was telling me a story about meeting someone new at Bible study, and I impatiently barked back a criticism of him. I was ungracious and unkind. I could shrug it off on not yet having my coffee, but the truth is I sinned against him. I needed to apologize. If one of my kids had stood up and said, 'I forgive you,' it would have been meaningless. They had no power to offer forgiveness in this situation. Josh was the offended party, and I needed his forgiveness. But my sin was also against God. I violated His commandment to be kind and tenderhearted toward one another. All of our sin is ultimately against God, and only He has the right ultimately to forgive.

Early in Jesus's ministry, we find Him in a house surrounded by such a thick crowd of people no one else could fit through the door. Armed with courage and creativity, four men carried their paralytic friend to the roof of the house, removed part of it, and lowered the helpless man down to Jesus in the hopes that he would be healed. Shocking everyone in the room, Jesus' first concern was not for the man's physical state, but his spiritual one. Speaking to this man's greatest need, Jesus' said, 'Your sins are forgiven.' The scribes who were present became enraged, thinking (rather ironically) to themselves that no one can forgive sins except God alone (Mark 2:1-12). They were right that God alone has the power to forgive sins; they were wrong to assume this power did not reside with Jesus.

Later in His ministry, Jesus declared the sins of a prostitute forgiven (Luke 7:48). And those of a dying thief on a cross beside His own (Luke 23:43). If Jesus were unable to forgive the sins of these people, He would have been in no better position to offer forgiveness than our children in the kitchen this morning. He would be a fraud – a horribly cruel liar, who deserves no respect or reverence in human history. But if He is actually able to forgive sins, He should be recognized as God in the flesh and worshiped.

JUDGE

As Jesus' popularity among the Jewish community grew and more people seriously contemplated His claims to be the Messiah, so also increasing was the religious elite's suspicion of Him. The Sadducees and Pharisees, usually at war with one another, joined forces to curb Jesus' influence by attempting to discredit Him. They knew of His audacious claims to be equal with God, and they sought to catch Him breaking one of the Jewish laws in order to show He was not on equal footing with God. They thought they had succeeded at cornering Him one day when He cured an invalid man on the Sabbath, the day the Jews were commanded to rest. Jesus responded to their opposition by stating, 'For as the Father raises the dead and gives them life, so also the Son gives life to whom he will' (John 5:21) The religious leaders wanted to catch Him breaking a Jewish sabbatical law. They didn't expect to catch Him fearlessly claiming to grant eternal life to whomever He wanted.

That was all the proof these men needed to show Jesus was speaking blasphemy. But Jesus had even more to say. 'For the Father judges no one, but has given all judgment to the Son, that all may honor the Son, just as they honor the Father.' (John 5:22-23). Claiming that He alone is judge of all people, Jesus said the Father gave this right to Him so that He would receive the same honor and worship that the Father does. Can you hear the horrified gasps of religious piety at hearing such a brazen claim by someone they already disdained? Jesus then continued, 'Whoever does not honor the Son does not honor the Father who sent him' (John 5:23). The indignation from the disapproving religious leaders in the crowd must have been visible by that point. They knew that by claiming judicial authority and honor, Jesus claimed rights that belong exclusively to God. They came looking to slyly prove He was not God; instead, Jesus declared openly His equality with God. Only a crazy person would claim to have the power to judge like God. That is, or someone who truly is God.

God's Name Given to Him

Historians refer to primary sources and secondary sources to categorize how close the writer was to the actual events they describe. All of the Gospels are primary-source materials. Matthew, Mark, Luke, and John were written by eyewitnesses or from interviews of people who were eyewitnesses to the events that happened. If the Old Testament builds a runway leading to the coming Messiah, the Gospels pull back the curtain and shine a spotlight on Jesus, authoritatively revealing Him to be the promised One who is God Himself.

The apostle John opens his Gospel in this way: 'In the beginning was the Word, and the Word was with God, and the Word was God' (John 1:1). This power-packed sentence opens this book, which was written so that readers 'might believe that Jesus is the Christ, the Son of God' (John 20:31). Before John tells his readers about the physical life and death of Jesus, John boldly claims the Word of God existed eternally, or as John (in reference to the Genesis creation account) calls it: 'in the beginning.'

To understand the significance of what John wrote, try to understand his commentary from the perspective of a first-century Jew familiar with the Old Testament. God had increasingly been revealing Himself to mankind throughout history using *words*. It was through *words* that God communicated to creation who He was. In Genesis 1 He spoke the universe into existence by using *words*. Later He spoke to Adam and Eve *words* that they understood. He gave Moses ten *words* (the Hebrew word for 'commandments' means 'words') that His people were to live by. Throughout the Old Testament, God gives *words* to prophets to lead His people. So closely does God identify with His words that His very presence was housed in the ark of the covenant, which held Moses' tablets containing the ten *words*. This God was present with His people through His *Word*.

John writes his Gospel aware that God had explicitly created, saved, ruled, and dwelt with His people by His Word. Understanding this background makes John's claim a few verses later even more glorious: 'And the Word became flesh and dwelt among us, and we have seen his glory, glory as of the only Son from the Father, full of grace and truth' (John 1:14). John wants his readers to be without any doubt that the Son of God has always existed as God and in deep, close, personal, and intimate union with God the Father. God's people had heard and obeyed His spoken Word and experienced His written Word, and now they were about to encounter His living Word.

John shows that just as the Word has been progressively unveiling God's character since creation, the supreme picture of God had arrived on earth in the person of Christ. Jesus is the ultimate and final revelation of the unseen God. As John writes at the end of his opening prologue, 'No one has ever seen God; the only God, who is at the Father's side, he has made him known' (John 1:18). The Son of God who existed in the very beginning with God the Father took on flesh and became man, Jesus Christ our Lord. John argues Jesus is the final climactic 'word' given to reveal to mankind who God is.

Mark also powerfully opens his biography of Jesus, explaining his intention to write, 'the gospel of Jesus Christ, the *Son of God.*' Mark wrote his firsthand account of the life of Jesus in large part to prove His divinity. In the first several chapters of his book, he shows Jesus uniquely has authority over nature, sickness, demons and He even has the power to forgive sins. The life and death of Jesus are described in detail over many chapters, but a key feature of the book we don't want to miss comes in the various ways Mark uses the title 'Son of God' to describe Jesus. It was the title pronounced on Jesus from heaven at both His baptism (Mark 1:11) and transfiguration (Mark 9:7). His divine Sonship was confessed by demons, who feared Jesus (Mark 3:11, 5:7). It was a title claimed by Jesus Himself before the High Priest (Mark 14:61-62). And in Mark 15 even the Roman officer guarding Jesus on the cross witnessed His death and proclaimed, 'Truly this man was the Son of God!' (Mark 15:39).

THE TRUE SON

It would be wise to stop briefly and address the term 'Son of God,' a phrase often found in Scripture, but not exclusively used there. For example, ancient Chinese kings and Egyptian pharaohs were often referred to as 'sons of god' or 'sons of heaven.' These early civilizations believed their leaders were direct descendants from their gods and should be feared as such; but, as polytheistic cultures they believed their rulers were sent from a god, not the one true God.

Within the pages of Scripture, this term was also used to mean different things in reference to different people. The label is used to describe angels as servants of God in Job 1; Adam as being directly created by God in Luke 3; the people of Israel corporately as God's chosen people in Exodus 4; and the Davidic king as God's special servant in 2 Samuel 7. In Jeremiah 3, God's sons refer to Israelites individually as intimately belonging to God. Even though the term is widely used in both history and Scripture, it finds its true fulfillment in only one person. Jesus was 'of God,' meaning of the same essence and substance as Yahweh. The term when used in Scripture to reference Jesus denotes His divinity.[3] It was only Jesus who perfectly fulfilled the term 'Son of God' in all that the name means: being of the same essence as the one true God. Many came

---

3   For more information, D.A. Carson's *Jesus: the Son of God* is an excellent resource.

before Him who represented different aspects of sonship, but all failed to live up to what it truly means to be *the* Son of God.

SECOND PERSON OF THE TRINITY

Immediately following John the Baptist's initial encounter with Jesus, John baptizes him. The Gospels record the same story that as Jesus came up from the water, the heavens opened, and the Spirit of God descended like a dove, resting on Jesus while a voice from heaven said, 'You are my beloved Son, with whom I am well pleased.'[4] This picture of the Trinity speaks to the divinity of Jesus. Simultaneous to the first public proclamation (by John the Baptist) that Jesus is the promised Messiah, God the Father and God the Holy Spirit present themselves united and pleased with Jesus. The Father announces publicly His affirmation for His Son, while the Spirit acts in harmony, empowering the ministry Jesus will soon undertake. This approval from heaven was repeated in front of three disciples during the transfiguration of Jesus when He appeared in radiant glory, speaking with Moses and Elijah: 'This is my beloved Son, which whom I am well pleased; listen to him.' (Matt. 17:1-13, Mark 9:2-13, Luke 9:28-36).

The Scriptures often speak of Jesus in unity with the Father and the Spirit. Jesus Himself commands His disciples to baptize His future believers in the name of the Father, Son, and Holy Spirit (Matt. 28:19). And Paul ends his second letter to the Corinthians: 'The grace of the Lord Jesus Christ and the love of God and the fellowship of the Holy Spirit be with you all' (2 Cor. 13:14). Jesus is referred to with the other persons of the Trinity, because Jesus is fully God.

---

4   Matthew 3:17, Mark 1:11, and Luke 3:22 all report practically identical narratives.

JESUS CALLED HIMSELF GOD

The names given to God in Scripture are sacred, and first century Jews would have treated them with honor. The Hebrew word for 'name' is *shem*, which literally means a position or reputation. In ancient culture, one's name described one's character. God's name carries such importance and holiness that the third of the ten commandments prohibited taking God's name in vain or intentionally misusing it.

We should understand this context when considering that Jesus referred to Himself by the holy and precious names of God. No sane person would have casually used God's name in reference to himself. He would have been committing the serious offense of blasphemy (punishable by death).

On one occasion Jesus had an extended debate with Jewish leaders about knowing God, and at the end of the conversation, He made the seemingly preposterous statement: 'Truly, truly, I say to you, before Abraham was, I am' (John 8:58). In this simple sentence Jesus claimed to be God. He said He existed before Abraham – 2,000 years before Jesus was born. And even more significantly, He called Himself by the personal name of God, 'I AM.' God had revealed Himself to Moses in the burning bush thousands of years earlier as 'I AM WHO I AM' (Exod. 3:1-17). 'I AM,' or Yahweh, was the sacred, personal, and unique name of the faithful God of the Hebrew people.

How did the Jews respond to Jesus' assertion? 'They picked up stones to throw at him.' Death by stoning was the sentence for blasphemy, and the Jews in the audience needed no further proof of Jesus' guilt. His claims to have authority from God and to forgive sins had them irate; but calling Himself the same name as God deserved immediate death. Scripture says, 'but Jesus hid himself and went out of the temple' (John 8:59). In fact, Jesus was accused of blasphemy for calling Himself equal with God several times (Matt. 26:65-66, Mark 2:6-7, Luke 5:21, Mark 14:63-64, Matt. 9:1-3).

Those who heard Jesus speak directly – as eyewitnesses – did not question whether He claimed to be God; they only questioned whether this man could possibly be telling the truth.

THE APOSTLES RECOGNIZED JESUS AS GOD

Forty years after Jesus' ascension to heaven, the early church was experiencing great persecution. Saul, in particular, was fervent and zealous in his fight against these followers of Christ. God intervened in a spectacular way in Saul's life, temporarily blinding his sight while opening his spiritual eyesight to see the truth of who Jesus is. After Saul's dramatic Damascus road conversion, he spent a few days with the disciples in that city before he spoke out publicly for the first time. What was the first thing this bully-turned-believer said publicly to explain his radical transformation? 'Immediately he proclaimed Jesus in the synagogues, saying, "He is the Son of God."' Because of his encounter with Jesus, a self-identified murder and persecutor of Christians turns 180 degrees and immediately calls Jesus divine.[5]

With Saul's corrected understanding of who Jesus was, he fervently set about telling others. He wanted the early church to be confident that the One they were worshiping and building their lives on was none less than God Himself. We know him best as the apostle Paul, and he wrote in the introduction of his letter to the Roman church that Jesus 'was declared to be the Son of God' (Rom. 1:4). In fact, throughout all thirteen Pauline epistles, he wrote consistently of Jesus as God. In his letter to the Colossians, he wrote of Jesus, 'He is the image of the invisible God' (Col. 1:15) in whom 'the whole fullness of deity dwells bodily' (Col. 2:9). The Greek word we translate as 'fullness' is *pleroma*, which implies an abundance of something. The whole fullness of God's nature dwells in Christ. More than just showcasing characteristics similar to God, Jesus embodies the 'Godness' of God. In Titus, Paul described Jesus

---

5   C.S. Lewis, *Mere Christianity* (London: Collins, first pub. 1952), pp. 36-37.

as 'our great God and Savior' (Titus 2:13). Paul boldly proclaimed Jesus to be God to every audience he held, starting from the very first one after his conversion and continuing his resolute proclamation throughout the known world. Persecution, beatings, and imprisonment couldn't stop Paul. He was eventually martyred for his message, but even that didn't stop him. His writings still speak today, proclaiming the deity of Christ.

Paul had company in his assertions about Jesus. The author of Hebrews wrote that Jesus 'is the radiance of the glory of God and the exact imprint of his nature' (Heb. 1:3). My children look a lot like me, but no one could claim we are the exact imprint of each other. An 'exact imprint' is not like a photocopy; rather, it is the exact expression of the thing. Jesus is the exact expression of God the Father, radiating His glory. The apostle Peter refers to Him as 'our God and Savior Jesus Christ' (2 Pet. 1:1). And Thomas, who had at one point doubted Jesus' bodily resurrection, touched the scars still present on the glorified body of Jesus and declared, 'My Lord and my God!' (John 20:28). The apostles would not have used these titles lightly, knowing the punishment for blasphemy was death. They were willing to risk their lives because they knew that Jesus, the One they had followed, is God.

Eternal Worship Due to Him

If Jesus is who He said He is, our response should be one of worship. He is God who became man in order to reconcile man to God. We should respond to this gracious God by calling Him Lord and falling at His feet in gratitude and worship. He is deserving of our adoration now and for all eternity. Predictably, this eternal worship is what the Bible both commands and foretells for Jesus.

Before history knew the name of Jesus, Isaiah wrote that man would worship Yahweh eternally. And this worship was reserved exclusively for Yahweh and none other. 'I am the LORD, that is my name; my glory I give to no other' (Isa. 42:8). And again Yahweh says: 'Turn to me and be saved, all the ends of the earth! For I am God, and there is no other. By myself I have sworn; from my mouth has gone out in righteousness a word that shall not return: To me every knee shall bow, every tongue shall swear allegiance' (Isa. 45:22-23). In other words, God said one day all the people on earth would confess salvation comes from Him and He alone is God. He will not share His glory with anyone else.

Paul used Isaiah's words in a letter to the church at Philippi, but notably he directed the worship to Jesus. 'Therefore God has highly exalted him and bestowed on him the name that is above every name, so that at the name of Jesus every knee should bow, in heaven and on earth and under the earth, and every tongue confess that Jesus Christ is Lord, to the glory of God the Father' (Phil. 2:9-11). Paul intentionally uses the same worshipful language God had reserved for Himself, but unapologetically ascribes this worship to Jesus, explaining this worship of Jesus will glorify God the Father.

Nowhere in Scripture do we see worship of Jesus as something the Father resents. In fact, the opposite is true. The Father encourages worship of His Son. In addition to the Philippians passage, the author of Hebrews writes, '[God] says, "Let all God's angels worship [the Son]"' (Heb. 1:6). The Father rejoices in the Son's worship because Jesus is God.

What will it look like to worship Jesus through all eternity? The aged apostle John, exiled to the island of Patmos for his faith, received special revelation meant to encourage the saints to persevere in the end times. It includes magnificent and majestic language about the worship of Jesus around the throne of God. John wrote, 'Then I looked, and I heard around the throne and the living creatures and the elders the voice of many angels, numbering myriads of myriads and thousands of thousands, saying with a loud voice, "Worthy is the Lamb who was slain, to receive power and wealth and wisdom and might and honor and glory and blessing!"' All the living creatures from the elders to the angels sing praises to Jesus. John continues, 'And I heard every creature in heaven and on earth and under the earth and in the sea, and all that is in them saying "To him who sits on the throne and to the Lamb be blessing and honor and glory and might forever and ever!" And the four living creatures said, "Amen!" and the elders fell down and worshiped' (Rev. 5:11-14). The elders worshiped on their faces. The creatures – all of them – worship in a unified chorus of praise to the only one worthy. And Jesus, the divine Lamb who was slain, sits on the throne of God forever and ever. He sits on the throne, because that seat is reserved for God.

No other option

In his classic book *Mere Christianity*, C. S. Lewis famously wrote that in light of all this evidence, people are left with only three possible choices to describe Jesus: as a liar, a lunatic, or Lord.

> You must make your choice. Either this man was, and is, the Son of God, or else a madman or something worse. You can shut him up for a fool, you can spit at him and kill him as a demon or you can fall at his feet and call him Lord and God, but let us not come with any patronising nonsense about his being a great human teacher. He has not left that open to us. He did not intend to. We are faced, then, with a frightening alternative. This man we are talking about either was (and is) just what He said or else a lunatic, or something worse. Now it seems to me obvious that He was neither a lunatic nor a fiend: and consequently, however strange or terrifying or unlikely it may seem, I have to accept the view that He was and is God.[6]

Jesus is not a fraud. He is no lunatic. He is the Son of God, eternal and equal to the Father, in full possession of all divine rights, characteristics, attributes, and worship.

---

6   Ibid, pp. 36-37.

Consider the list of those who claimed Jesus was God or attested to His divinity: God the Father, God the Holy Spirit, Jesus Himself, Old Testament prophets, the disciples who lived with Jesus, and other New Testament writers. Even the demons knew Jesus was God and feared Him (Mark 1:23-24). In other words, all the spiritual world and the inspired writers of Scripture over thousands of years and multiple contexts, cultures, nations, and languages, spoke in harmony that Jesus was God. Jesus wasn't merely a good man or a moral teacher or a revolutionary. The Scriptures themselves leave us with no other alternative: Jesus is God.

QUESTIONS

FULLY GOD

Without divine revelation of the truth of who Jesus is, we may be tempted to believe He was something less than the divine Son of God. When comprehensively surveying the evidence found in Scripture, however, we can have confidence that before Jesus was from Nazareth, He was ruling the universe from heaven as God. The roll call of those who testify to His divine Sonship is both comprehensive and authoritative. Jesus was prophesied from ancient times to be God. He acted like God. He was called by the holy names of God. And Scripture promises He will be worshiped for all eternity as being God. Those who spoke with authority about the life of Jesus claimed in unison that He was divine: God the Father, the Spirit, Jesus Himself, the ancient prophets, His disciples, and other New Testament writers.

1. How would Sophia's (p. 35) life change if she believed Jesus is God?

2. Other religions teach that Jesus was not God, and yet 2,000 years after His death, people all over the world still study His life, memorize His words, and obey His teachings. What are some claims you have heard (or wrestled with yourself) about Jesus' identity?

3. Despite both the passages in Isaiah (7:14, 9:6, 40:3) that predicted the Messiah would be God and the signs Jesus performed in front of crowds of people, many people did not believe He was divine. Why would this belief have been so unpopular in Jesus' day? Are those reasons still around today?

4. God has certain privileges and powers that no creature has, yet Jesus possesses these attributes. Christians have the ability to

reflect some of these divine attributes of God without actually possessing them. What is the difference between Jesus having these attributes and our reflecting God's attributes?

5. When God revealed Himself to Moses in the burning bush, He called Himself 'I AM WHO I AM.' (Exod. 3:1-17). In the narrative found in John 8:56-59, Jesus refers to Himself as 'I AM,' this personal and holy name for God. Why did the Jews pick up stones to throw at Jesus? Did these Jews question whether or not Jesus claimed to be God? How would you use this account to show a friend that Jesus claimed to be God?

6. The Biblical writers were well aware of the serious offense they would be committing if they called a mere man by the name of God. And yet in practically every letter they wrote they use beautifully descriptive divine language in referring to Jesus. Write down some of the names the writers of the New Testament use in reference to Jesus. (Some are found in John 20:28, Rom. 1:4, Phil. 2:6, Col. 1:15, Titus 2:13, Heb. 1:3) Why would they have had such confidence that Jesus is God?

7. Isaiah predicted that Yahweh would receive worship for delivering His people from their sins (Isaiah 44:23), and the New Testament explicitly and unapologetically ascribes this worship as belonging to Jesus. Revelation describes a scene happening in heaven where everything from elders to angels are singing praise. Read Revelation 5:1-14. What does this passage tell us about Jesus? How does it affirm that Jesus is God?

8. In your own words, tell how you would explain to a friend why you believe Jesus is fully God.

Chapter 3

From Him, Through Him, and To Him

Dana is a stay at home mom who has struggled off and on for years with depression. Lately she seems unable to find any light at all in life. She finds no joy in her young children and in the bottomless list of chores they create. Her marriage feels stale, and she is wondering if there is any reason for her life. She always thought she would find joy and happiness in her family. Instead she feels lonely, empty, and without purpose. She came to women's Bible study this week as a last-ditch effort to see if there were any answers to be found to her big questions, and she has struck up a conversation with you. She asks you what purpose you have in living. What do you tell her?

In the early fourth century the theologian Arius taught that Jesus was close to God, but not on par with *the* God. He argued that Jesus was the greatest of all creatures, but He was still created by God. And, therefore, there was a time when He did not exist. Arius intentionally pitted the eternal Father against the Son, whom he argued had a beginning. According to Arius, Jesus was sent by God on a divine errand to complete a checklist of tasks necessary to accomplish salvation for mankind. In their zeal to separate the Son from God the Father, Arius and his followers wrote a catchy tune distinguishing the two. The translated version of the song goes something like this:

> And so God Himself, as he really is, is inexpressible to all.
> He alone has no equal, no one similar, and no one of the same glory.
> We call Him unbegotten, in contrast to him who by nature is begotten.
> We praise him as without beginning, in contrast to him who has a beginning.
> We worship him as timeless, in contrast to him who in time came to exist.[1]

It is hard to imagine belting out this song in the shower or getting it stuck in your head all day, but it became such a popular tune that people sang it even as they traveled. This false idea about Jesus being less than God seemed plausible to many and spread quickly throughout the known world.

Could Christianity exist with a Jesus who is a lesser god? Mormons and Jehovah's Witnesses believe so. Unitarians don't accept the deity of Jesus. What do we lose in relegating Jesus to a lesser status except contentious debate? Is there truth to Arius' claim that Jesus is close but not quite God, or is there at least a benefit to embracing the position that Jesus' divinity is irrelevant to our faith?

Fortunately, the early church dealt head-on with Arius' false teaching, labeling it heresy. As we saw in chapter 2 scripture is clear that Jesus is God, and we gain nothing by ignoring this truth. Conversely, a careful examination of the divinity of Jesus leads to new avenues of delight and worship in Him. In a later chapter on

---

1   Aaron J. West, *'Arius – Thalia in Greek and English'. Fourth Century Christianity.* Wisconsin Lutheran College. Retrieved 16 August 2016.

how salvation was accomplished, we will explore the necessity that Jesus is God for us to be reconciled to Him. For now, pausing to focus only on His divinity and its implications gives us opportunity to know Him better and as a result, worship Him more truly. Intentionally slowing down to linger as we observe the deity of Jesus should be satisfying for our souls. One day the family of God will gather together and behold the glory and majesty of Christ in full. While we wait, we have confidence Jesus is to be exalted above all other things, just as the Romans doxology declares: 'For from him and through him and to him are all things. To him be glory forever' (Rom. 11:36).

Without exception my favorite meal of the year is the Thanksgiving dinner we eat with our multi-national church body as we celebrate together God's kindness in giving us Himself and each other. This past year by lunchtime on Thanksgiving Day, my youngest daughter was overwhelmed by the anticipation of the feast that was to come. She observed it all – the smells, the buzz of activity, her father's occasional outburst of 'I'm so thankful for turkey!' To help her wait for the meal, I let her sample a few dishes. It fed her desire to feast on the meal that was to come later that day, and it also whet her appetite for more. That small plate of food did not fill her, and she did not taste everything that was later to be on the table. But she got a good sample of what was coming, and that simultaneously helped her wait and also made her look forward to the meal even more.

In eternity we will feast, knowing God's glory fully and in a manner that never ends; for now, we sample an appetizer, considering how meditating on Jesus's divinity can lead us to greater worship: from Him, through Him, and to Him.

From Him: the Eternal Son of God

From eternity past, before Jesus was ever born in Bethlehem or lived as a carpenter in Galilee, God the Son existed, and Jesus – this

Son – will continue to exist as God for all eternity. Eternal existence is a difficult concept for us to comprehend, since our only frame of reference is the regular rhythm and passage of time. But Scripture uses a variety of metaphors and language to explain the eternality of Christ. The Old Testament prophet Micah predicted the Messiah would be 'from of old, of ancient days' (Micah 5:2). The author of Hebrews said He has 'neither beginning of days nor end of life.' (Heb. 7:3). Revelation describes Him as the 'Alpha and the Omega, the first and last, the beginning and the end' (Rev. 22:13). Jesus Himself confirmed His eternal existence as God multiple times when He was on earth. On the night before His crucifixion He asked the Father to 'glorify me in your presence with the glory I had with you before the world began' (John 17:5). Contrary to Arius' teaching, Jesus had no beginning, and He will have no ending. The implications of the eternality of Christ are enormous for us. The blood of the eternal Son of God was required as payment for our sin. How costly was the gift that he offers us freely! Because our salvation is given from the eternal God, it is a gift that will last forever.

THE KING WHO LEFT HIS THRONE

In my Middle Eastern town, it is common to see pictures of our rulers in public places. You cannot go shopping, pick up your laundry, or drive down the road without seeing pictures of our ruling sheiks. Their pictures communicate that they have power and authority over all the land. Their powerful positions require they exercise governing responsibilities, but it also means they enjoy many unique privileges. They live in palaces and have staff that meet their needs. People under their rule recognize their authority and honor them for it. It is practically unfathomable to think that a powerful sheikh would intentionally step down off his throne, forfeit his rights as king, and choose to live among the poor in the slums.

But listen to Paul's description of what Jesus did: 'He did not count equality with God a thing to be grasped, but emptied himself, by taking the form of a servant, being born in the likeness of men' (Phil. 2:6-7). The Son of God had been enjoying divine privileges eternally – fully satisfied and content as angels attended to Him and worshiped Him, perfectly enjoying relationship in the Trinity and all the glory that is due Him as God. He owned the cattle on a thousand hills (Ps. 50:10). But Jesus did not cling to His rights as God. He laid those rights aside and emptied himself to be like a lowly servant.

Had Jesus only lived on earth as a man for a short period before ascending back to heaven, that would deserve our awe. If the ruler of my city were to go visit a poor neighborhood for an afternoon, the newspapers would report on his trip and people would talk about what a benevolent and kind ruler he is. But Jesus did significantly more. He left His eternal throne to be born as an infant dependent on His human mother. He didn't just visit a poor neighborhood; He made his home there. He grew up to eventually die a cruel, painful, humiliating death in the place of sinful, rebellious people. This is far more incomprehensible than a finite earthly king forfeiting his crown to live like a common man.

What would cause Jesus to do such a radical thing? Paul tells the Philippians that Jesus became man to die on the cross to pay for our sins, carrying out the will of God. Our sin is so great that it required the blood payment of an eternal God. It was our rebellion that led Him to leave His heavenly home and suffer on our behalf. While we often prefer to think of our sins as simple mistakes or mere detours from the ideal course, God says our sin makes us His enemy, and it elicits in Him a righteous fury. The Old Testament prophet Nahum said, 'the LORD takes vengeance on his adversaries and keeps wrath for his enemies' (Nahum 1:2). Do you think God's wrath is only for bad people, and your relatively small sins can't possibly ignite God's fury? God's response to all sin is now and always has been a righteous anger.

So what punishment is sufficient to pay the debt you owe as God's enemy? Many religions offer answers to these questions. They tell us to make up for our rebellion by doing good deeds. Help those in need. Say a set of religious words. Fast and pray. Be kind. Meditate. Go to church/temple/mosque.

Imagine a convict sitting on death row of a prison for rape and murder. He offers the victim's family a quilt he sewed for them and expects a pardon in return. The state would not be swayed by his gesture, even if it were done with great sincerity, because it isn't an adequate payment for the crime committed. Likewise, when we try to offer God our own righteous deeds in an attempt to earn His favor, He tells us they are 'like filthy rags.' (Isa. 64:6 NIV). Eve's fig leaves were insufficient to cover her nakedness. Our 'righteous deeds' are no different.

In order to answer this question in truth, we must understand that God stands in a category alone. Our sin ultimately is committed against Him, and it is His wrath that must be satisfied before sins can be forgiven. But only God Himself is big enough to absorb His wrath and not face eternal destruction. His punishment would never be satisfied but would last forever if it landed anywhere other than Himself. In other words, God the Father's wrath against sin went out and – in the cross of Christ – landed on God the Son. It had to if He were going to redeem sinful people.

Punishment for God's enemies looks like a Roman cross, where the Son of God died for those in rebellion against Him. Jesus died so that rebels could be reconciled to God. 'While we were still sinners, Christ died for us' (Rom. 5:8). How costly the gift was that He offers us freely! From Him come all things, including salvation.

When I take time to meditate on the magnitude of God Himself paying the eternal debt I owe, my delight in my Savior soars (even higher than my daughter's at her first bite of Thanksgiving pie). There is nothing I can do to pay for my sins. The punishment I deserve for my sins is eternal, and only God could pay the penalty for me. He freely did so in the person of Jesus Christ. So serious is our sin that the King of the universe left His throne and died a humiliating death for it. And so serious is God's love that He willingly did it.

ETERNAL RELATIONSHIP

Jesus' eternality will either bring us great comfort or great fear because our acceptance or rejection of Him has eternal consequences. For those who are in Christ, an eternity with Jesus awaits. The greatest gift He offers mankind is Himself, and He gives us an eternity to enjoy it, to enjoy *Him*.

As a child, the concept of *for-ev-er* was terrifying for me. I hated even thinking about how something could *never* end. I likened eternity to a mundane day on repeat. I assumed it must be like the movie *Groundhog Day,* a nightmarish repeat of the exact same day with no end in sight; except unlike the movie, eternity had no closing credits. Even a really good day surrounded by people I really liked would eventually get tiresome, and I reasoned eternity would be a place I would grow bored and yet never be able to escape. Truthfully, my idea of heaven seemed more like prison than the freedom and joy promised in Scripture.

Thankfully, my elementary understanding of eternal life is not at all what heaven is like. Instead, imagine something as complex as the universe of planets and stars. Mankind's knowledge of the vast universe is minuscule, and yet scientists devote their lives to studying the fraction of information currently available to us. Imagine if a scientist had unhindered access to every part of the universe. How long it would take to discover and observe every aspect of the creation! It would take centuries, even millennia to study the stars, each individual and unique planet and their moons, the solar systems, the galaxies, the comets, the constellations, the black holes, and aspects of the universe we do not even yet know exist. Now consider that the writer of Genesis barely mentions the stars. It appears they are almost an afterthought when he writes about creation. Genesis 1:16 records, 'And God made the two great lights – the greater light to rule the day and the lesser light to rule the night – *and the stars*.'

The One who created the universe is far more vast and amazing than His creation. While the entirety of the universe seems almost incomprehensible to the human mind, it did not even get its own sentence in creation week. Heaven will give us free access to study and admire God forever. He is infinitely vast, and His nature and His ways are known only in part to us now. But when we have all of eternity to explore and grow in our understanding of God, there will not be a boring day.

The Westminster Catechism has taught us the purpose of our lives is to 'know God and enjoy him forever.' That is what all men and women were created by God to do. We grow in our *enjoyment* of God when we grow in our *knowledge* of Him. The more we know Him, the more we enjoy Him. In heaven, when we have unhindered access to the God of the universe, our enjoyment will never end. We will be fully satisfied because we are fully doing what we were created to do – without the impediments caused by our sin. We will live eternally with Him in full satisfaction of Him. 'In your presence there is fullness of joy; at your right hand are pleasures forevermore' (Ps. 16:11).

But for those who are not in Christ, the sobering reality is that an eternity in hell awaits. Hell is not merely the absence of God; it is the presence of God in His holy, unmediated wrath. It is a place of eternal damnation, separation from God's mercy, and punishment for sin. Scripture describes it as a 'fiery lake of burning sulfur' (Rev. 21:8), the 'realm of the dead' (Ps. 9:17), 'everlasting destruction' (2 Thess. 1:9), a 'blazing furnace, where there will be weeping and gnashing of teeth' (Matt. 13:50), 'where the fire never goes out' (Mark 9:43), and where there are 'chains of darkness' (2 Pet. 2:4). Those descriptions are sufficient to show it is a place of great suffering and punishment intentionally inflicted on rebellious humans by a just God. Every single sin ever committed in the history of the world will be punished. Either a substitute will bear God's wrath for your sins, or you will bear the wrath of God for each of your sins in hell for eternity.

The grievous fact of hell can sometimes feel intolerable to us. We often hesitate to speak of God's judgment in hell, even when proclaiming the gospel to non-Christians. It can be an awkward and uncomfortable concept for those who understand God to be loving and forgiving.

The good news is that no one has to go to hell. Through Jesus, God has accomplished salvation and has freely opened heaven and eternity with Him for those who repent of their sins and trust in Him. The bad news is that many will reject this rescue plan in favor of the futile attempted coup against God. In his classic work *Knowing God*, J. I. Packer writes, 'Nobody stands under the wrath of God except those who have chosen to do so. The essence of God's action in wrath is to give men what they choose, in all its implications: nothing more, and equally nothing less. God's readiness to respect human choice to this extent may appear disconcerting and even terrifying, but it is plain that his attitude here is supremely just...'[2] God's extravagant efforts to save men from His wrath are evident when we look at the cross. Unfortunately, many will foolishly forgo God's grace in favor of His wrath.

Through Him: the Creator and Sustainer of All

Scripture teaches the Son of God is the One through whom all things were created. In describing the preeminence of Christ, Paul writes: 'For by him all things were created, in heaven and on earth,

---

2   J. I. Packer, *Knowing God* (London: IVP, 1993), p. 153.

visible and invisible, whether thrones or dominions or rulers or authorities – all things were created through Him and for Him. And He is before all things...' (Col. 1:16-17). John also wrote, 'All things were made through him, and without him was not anything made that was made' (John 1:3). The language is comprehensive – all things. All things were created through the Son and for the Son. People, animals, and all creation were created through Him and for Him. The physical world we can see and the spiritual world we cannot see were created through Him and for Him. Nations, kings, and authority structures were created through Him and for Him. And ultimately, you were created through Him and for Him.

This is why He was able to quiet the winds and the waves and walk on water. He created that sea; He could control it. This is why He was able to turn water into wine. He created hydrogen and oxygen and put them together. He created vines and grapes. It was no effort for Him to change the molecules from one to another. This is also how He multiplied fish and fed over 5,000 people from five loaves of bread. He created all that swim in the seas and all the grain that grows in the fields. He certainly could produce enough to feed the hungry crowds. Who but God could do these things?

OUT OF NOTHING

With the magnificent act of creation, the Son displayed His creativity, His orderliness, and His vast power. He spoke and things that did not previously exist came into existence. As the universe was formed with the words of God by the Word of God, it displayed creation's obedience to Him. It demonstrated His magnificence and His glory. The created universe was not chaotic or disorderly, but rather it was created 'good.' Theologians refer to the creation as *ex nihilo*, meaning 'out of nothing.' This phrase merely means the universe was not sculpted out of existing material. Observing creation from this standpoint allows us to see that God is separate from the rest of creation. There is a clear distinction between the divine and the created. God, as the Creator, is the absolute owner of all the heavens and the earth. Nothing exists apart from His will for it to exist.

I can remember hiking through the Alps with my husband and gasping out loud at the beauty before us. Once when we were in the Cayman Islands visiting friends, we were snorkeling, and I was completely overwhelmed at the beauty of God's creation that existed under the sea. Under the sea! Only a few people around us were enjoying the same view we were, and I couldn't help but wonder what other beautiful parts of creation existed in places humans have never been. When we gaze at the beauty, vastness, and diversity of God's creation, we can hardly help but feel small in comparison. Even agnostic friends have admitted feeling disoriented in these moments when they are looking for something or someone to thank for nature, something to praise for such a beautiful world. In the moment of taking in the magnificence and beauty of something so great, it feels insufficient to think about this world coming into existence accidentally. That's because it didn't. Jesus is the one to thank and praise for the beauty we see.

Sustainer

The eternal Son not only created this world and everything in it, but He is also sustaining this world and all the things in it. Looking again at Colossians we find that, 'he is before all things, and in him all things hold together' (Col. 1:17). Hebrews 1:3 declares, 'He upholds the universe by the word of his power.' Contrary to those who have argued throughout history that God passively watches creation, the Son of God is actively holding all things together. Not a single molecule in the universe is independent of the power and authority of Jesus.

Does this knowledge bring you comfort? In our broken world of war, heartache and injustice, we can find peace and rest knowing that the One through whom all things were created is the same

One who sustains His creation as well. He is not distant; He is actively ruling over His creation. Nothing happens apart from His gracious sovereignty. This is why we can come confidently to Him in prayer. He has control over all things. We don't even have to fear suffering because we know it comes for our good and His glory, for He 'works all things according to the counsel of his will' (Eph. 1:11; see also Rom. 8:28). Prone to worry? Know that you can cast 'all your anxieties on him, because he cares for you' (1 Peter 5:7). Comfort comes from knowing the One who loves us holds the whole world in His hands.

To Him: Our Purpose is His Glory

Far from the impersonal purposeless view of the universe that is held by many, the Scriptures reveal that the act of creation was a personal act. All things were made with a purpose and for a person. That person is Jesus. 'All things were created through him *and for him*' (Col. 1:16). All things fulfill their purpose as they reach their goal of relating rightly to God through Jesus.

This includes you. According to the Bible, you were created not just by but also for Jesus. You are known by Him because He created you. And you were intentionally created for a purpose – for Him. This means in order to find *our* purpose in life, we must submit to Jesus. Ironically, we will only know real freedom in life when we give our lives over to Him. This is why dying to self means life and freedom in Christ. Jesus said, 'For whoever would save his life will lose it, but whoever loses his life for my sake and the gospel's sake will save it' (Mark 8:35). Until we give over our lives to Jesus, we are in bondage to something other than that for which we were made.

God made us with a capacity to know joy, and yet we can only perfectly be satisfied in Him. This world is full of temptations calling out and luring us to find joy in inferior things, but our lives are to be lived for the purpose for which God created us – to know Him and glorify Him.

A race car is designed for precise and fast driving. Its engine is designed to accelerate quickly and maintain high levels of speed. Its wheels are positioned for quick maneuvering and fast turns. Its aerodynamic design limits wind resistance and helps maximize speed. Of course, if I had a race car, I could drive it to the grocery store. I could park it outside my house and turn the radio on to listen to while I work in the garden. The neighborhood cat could take a nap under it. Those are fine things, but they don't fulfill the purpose for which that car was made.

Similarly, but at a much deeper level, you were made with purpose. You were carefully designed by and hand-crafted for Jesus. Until you submit your life to Him, you are driving groceries around in a race car. Your life was made for a greater purpose.

So many people on this planet are living for mediocre things: jobs, money, hobbies, families, entertainment. Spending an entire life in pursuit of advancing a career or collecting nice things will never satisfy. C.S. Lewis argued that the problem is not that we are lured away from finding our purpose in life by more enjoyable things, but that we are actually tempted away by far lesser ones. He said, 'It would seem that Our Lord finds our desires not too strong, but too weak. We are half-hearted creatures, fooling about with drink and sex and ambition when infinite joy is offered us, like an ignorant child who wants to go on making mud pies in a slum because he cannot imagine what is meant by the offer of a holiday at the sea. We are far too easily pleased.'[3] The problem is not the things that tempt us away; the problem is with our desires.

Jesus offers us a new identity in Himself. He offers us an invitation to be a daughter of the King with all the rights, privileges and responsibilities that come with it. He offers us so much more than 'drink and sex and ambition.' He offers us more than hobbies

---

3   C. S. Lewis, *The Weight of Glory* (New York City, NY: HarperCollins, 2001), p. 26.

and jobs and families. What God freely offers us is an eternal relationship with our Creator and the ability to glorify Him. When we find our identity and fulfillment in the place where we were intended to find it, we find a freedom only known to those who are in Christ. With that new identity and freedom, we are able to take on a godly ambition at work without letting it consume us. We are able to enjoy our hobbies, giving thanks to God. And we are able to serve our families, knowing that God has given them to us to enjoy and to point to Christ for His glory. These things are no longer our purpose in life. They are merely the means by which we enjoy The Purpose. When we are new creatures with new identities, bringing God glory is what brings us satisfaction and delight.

In and through Jesus, God offers us free access behind the curtain to the Creator and Sustainer of all things. We are made in His image to know and love Him. Those who reject Him will never know the true freedom they were made to know. Those who love and follow Jesus know joy and fulfillment in life even whether we are suffering through a trial or in the midst of very ordinary and sometimes mundane duties. The Christian knows this life is preparation for the next, when we have all eternity to be with our Creator fulfilling our glorious purpose of knowing and loving our Savior. To Him are all things!

God of God, Light of Light, Very God of Very God

Led by Athanasius, fourth-century theologians recognized Arius' teaching as unbiblical, rose up, and called him a heretic. Division broke out, and in an effort to bring unity, the emperor called for the council of Nicaea in 325 to settle this dispute about the nature of Jesus. At this council, bishops focused on what Scripture taught about the nature of Jesus. (An interesting historical asterisk is that allegedly during one of these meetings, St. Nicholas – of Santa Claus fame – punched Arius in the face because he was so enraged by Arius' blasphemous comments about Jesus not being

God. Maybe St. Nick was not so jolly when it came to heresy!) The bishops drew a line in the sand: They concluded that any statements that fell short of Jesus being both fully God and fully man were heresy and anyone who taught such was to be labeled a heretic. Out of this counsel came the Nicene Creed describing the Lord Jesus Christ as the Son of God, 'God of God, Light of Light, very God of very God; begotten, not made, being of one substance with the Father, by whom all things were made.'

Jesus is God. The Scriptures testify to this fact from beginning to end. Arius, in the fourth century, and all of his progeny since, are wrong. It is only God who can save. 'For from him and through him and to him are all things. To him be glory forever! Amen' (Rom. 11:36).

QUESTIONS

FROM HIM, THROUGH HIM, AND TO HIM

As God, Jesus is the source of all things. All things are from Him and through Him and to Him. He is eternal. He is the creator of all things. He sustains all things. And all things are made for His glory. These big truths about Christ affect our mundane everyday lives on earth in big and glorious ways.

1. How can grasping the reality of Jesus' divinity give Dana (p. 63) purpose in life?

2. We often prefer to think of our sins as simple mistakes or mere detours from the ideal course, but God says otherwise. How does God describe sin and His attitude toward it? (Read Nahum 1:2 and Romans 2:5)

3. How should understanding our sin as rebellion against the eternal God affect our posture toward God and our attitude toward sin?

4. In light of the lengths that the eternal king of the universe went to in order to rescue us from our sins, why are the efforts of other religions to punish sin so ineffective? Do you have a view of sin that matches what Christ Jesus had to do because of it, or do you have a small view of sin? Are you regularly considering your own life and searching for sin to destroy? (Ps. 139:23)

5. Another group of created beings also sinned against God. And yet He did not choose to redeem them. Read 2 Peter 2:4. What happened to these beings?

6. Read Ephesians 2:1-9. Why should we as Christians be marked by humility? Explain why God is described in this passage as

being 'rich in mercy.' What do you see in this passage that we will see more clearly in heaven?

7. Ephesians 2:7 describes the immeasurable riches of His grace as displayed in the *kindness* of Christ Jesus. His free gift of salvation is the most obvious display of this characteristic. Are there other areas of your life where you do not believe Jesus has been kind to you? Pray that God would allow you to see and believe this characteristic of Jesus is true in all aspects of your life.

8. The concept of an eternal hell can be uncomfortable for us. Some passages that describe it are Revelation 21:8, Psalm 9:17, 2 Thessalonians 1:9, Matthew 13:50, Mark 9:43, and 2 Peter 2:4. In your own words, explain why hell is a just punishment from God.

9. Not only did Jesus create all things, He holds all things together (Col. 1:17). Not a single molecule in the universe is independent of the power and authority of Jesus. Therefore, we understand each of us was made by Jesus for a purpose and intention. If we were made by Him and for Him, where will we find ultimate rest and satisfaction? Where are you tempted to look for rest and satisfaction? How do those things and places stack up next to your Creator? Why are we so tempted by lesser things?

10. Jesus is actively sustaining all things, including your life. Are there ways you see your life disconnected from this truth? How are you tempted to slip into thinking your life is disconnected from Jesus?

11. Does your knowledge that Jesus has ultimate authority in your life bring comfort or fear?

Chapter 4

Fully Man

Noura is a mother of three and is pregnant with her fourth. She and her husband just found out their new baby boy has a genetic disorder and if he survives the pregnancy, he probably won't live to reach his first birthday. She is angry with God and sees no purpose in her innocent son suffering. She is beginning to question whether there really is a God at all. She has asked you to coffee to talk about her struggles. How can you encourage her?

I was in high school when I first noticed my eyesight was less than 20/20. Back then, using technology in the classroom meant that a box-shaped TV and a VCR was wheeled in on a pushcart from the storage room, so most of our class work was still written on a whiteboard at the front of the room. I realized one day I was squinting to see what my peers seemed to be copying from the board with ease, so my mom made an appointment at the local optometrist.

Driving home after my doctor's visit, my eyes adjusting to a new pair of contact lenses, I was shocked at how many details in the world around me I had been missing. The flowers were not just blobs of color, but suddenly they had individual petals. The trees were not just outlines of green, but had actual leaves – and I could see each one. I remember slowing down to look at a particular oak tree close to my house and marveling at how beautiful it was. Have you ever thought tree bark was beautiful? That day, I did. I had passed that tree every day for 16 years, but I had never even stopped to look at it, much less appreciate the detail of it.

Likewise, sometimes we don't enjoy the beauty of Christ's incarnation because we don't see it clearly. We lack understanding of what it means that the eternal God humbled Himself by taking on flesh, subjecting Himself to the limitations of physical life and death, and rising again to exist forever as both fully God and fully man. Sometimes we don't marvel at this beautiful aspect of Jesus' existence because we simply don't slow down to gaze at it. We have clear vision, but that which is common to us, much like that oak tree near my house, does not seize our attention. The incarnation of Jesus seems about as powerful and relevant as the plastic baby in a tiny manger surrounded by toy animals we pull out of the closet each December. It might be sweet and mildly interesting to look at, but we're not particularly impressed.

Pastor Sinclair Ferguson helps reorient our thinking about the man Christ Jesus when he says, 'If your intellect has never been staggered by the reality of the incarnation, you don't know what the incarnation means. It doesn't mean Jesus was a little baby. It means the eternal, infinite, divine One, worshiped by Cherubim and Seraphim, the Creator of all things, the sustainer of all things, infinite in His being, wisdom, power, majesty, and glory – who in a word could dissolve the world that had sinned against Him – was willing to come into this world and assume our flesh in order to become our Savior. It is overwhelming. That's the great thing about the gospel.'[1]

Jesus, the Perfect Man

Before we focus on the humanity of Jesus, we should consider the seemingly simple question: What does it mean to be human? While agreeing on the definition of *humanity* sounds like an easy exercise, history proves otherwise. Some have argued that being human is synonymous with mistake: 'To err is human,' they say. Some have stood by reason as the chief definition of humanity: 'I think; therefore, I am.' Postmodernists differ, arguing all knowledge is merely a collection of one's individual discourse. They say there is no unified human nature to define us. Instead, they argue, being human is different for each person. Evolutionary scientists also offer an answer to the question of what makes us human. They say we are a scientific classification of *homo sapiens*, a specific category of living organisms. But, of course, biological categories can speak nothing to purpose of life or the deep spiritual longing almost all humans experience. I polled my own children one morning to see what they thought made humans unique among the rest of the animal kingdom. After a moment of consideration, one of my daughters astutely said, 'We brush our hair, and they don't.'

In the midst of a world with varying answers and definitions, the best place to find out what humans were intended to be is to look to the creator of them. Twenty-six verses into the Bible's account of the creation of the world, God turns His attention toward *adam*, the Hebrew word for *mankind*. We learn about all of God's plan for mankind as He gives instructions to this one particular man – this son of God – aptly named Adam. Importantly, God gave Adam (and thus all of *adam*) dominion over the earth. What's more, God declared that mankind was created *in His own image*,

---

1   Sinclair Ferguson, 2011 Ligonier National Conference, Light & Heat: A Passion for the Holiness of God. 'Why the God-Man.'

both male and female (Gen. 1:27). Mankind was blessed by God and was commanded to multiply and take care of God's creation. With abundance, God gave humans everything that was needed for life, and God was pleased with His creation.

Fundamental to our comprehensive understanding of what it means to be human is understanding that we were created by God. That may sound basic, but the competing understandings (or lack thereof) of what it means to be human demonstrate that this essential fact isn't just overlooked but is rejected by our world. God tells us in Scripture that *He* 'breathed into [man's] nostrils the breath of life' (Gen. 2:7b). Rightly understanding humanity involves a knowledge that we have a creator who had purpose in creating us. We are accountable to Him and under His authority. God made us unique from the other animals and living organisms on earth because He made us in his 'own image.'

Being made in the image of God means we are something akin to a portrait – not as good or as accurate as the real thing, but nonetheless a picture of the real thing. God created human beings with a very high purpose and calling: to be His representatives on earth. We were made 'a little lower than the angels' in our assignment to steward the earth and all that is in it, yet God crowned His people with 'glory and honor' (Ps. 8:5). As God's agents on earth, tending to His creation, Adam and Eve were meant to know and enjoy God and all that He made, including unfiltered, unmediated, direct access to Him.

Therefore, a comprehensive definition of humanity as it was intended by God involves an acceptance that we were made to be God's creatures, exhibiting His image, stewarding His creation, being in perfect communion with Him, and living obediently under His good authority. Everything was perfect in the Garden of Eden as God initially created it and declared it to be good – including humans. But sadly, everything changed for Adam and Eve and the rest of humanity on that dark day when sin entered our world. The image of God we bore was from then on marred. Our communion with Him was broken. Our stewardship of His creation was made far more difficult. So, in a sense, to err is not human – in the original definition of the word. But to err is certainly *fallen* human.

The Son of God, fully divine to be worshiped for eternity, was sent from God the Father to be fully man, as man was intended by God to be. Jesus fulfilled all the expectations of this true humanity – showcasing the image of God, stewarding His creation, knowing perfect communion with God, and living obediently under His good authority. From His birth to His death, Jesus lived a fully human life – even though His life was anything but ordinary. As the One designated by God to fulfill the rescue plan promised to Adam and Eve after the fall, we see both Jesus' full humanity and His specific calling. He was from the seed of the woman but he had the unique task to crush the head of the serpent (Gen. 3:15). The recorded events of His life show He was like us, yet altogether unique from us.

GOOD NEWS OF GREAT JOY

Scripture provides a significant amount of detail surrounding the birth of Jesus. Let's review some of the facts we know. His family tree is included in the Gospels (Luke 3:23-38). His mother Mary was betrothed to marry Joseph when she found out she was pregnant. Scripture reveals they had to travel to Bethlehem shortly before Jesus' birth because of a census being taken by Caesar Augustus to count all the people under Roman rule. This decree ordered everyone to return to their family's hometown. Mary and Joseph had been living in Nazareth but traveled to Bethlehem, the city of Joseph's family (the household of David) (Luke 2:1-5). We also know Bethlehem was crowded with all the visitors who had come back to town for the census, making it difficult for Mary to find a private place to give birth (Luke 2:7).

These details provided by Scripture tell us a good bit of information about the physical birth of the baby Jesus, and help us see He is like us, yet unique from us. In one sense, His birth was similar to every other baby born in the world. The time came for Mary to give birth, she felt pain, she labored for a while, and then in time she delivered a baby boy. He certainly cried, and Mary probably swaddled Him and let Him sleep. In that sense, Jesus' birth was a fairly ordinary event.

But there were extraordinary and supernatural details tightly woven into this narrative – the prophecy, the virgin birth, the star, the angels. No one else has had a birth like this one, and His unique birth was meant to draw the attention it did. He was born from a woman in the same way all men are, but He was born from the womb of a virgin. The birth of Jesus in this supernatural way was a sign that this baby's life would not be like everyone else's. One of us, but very unique from us.

Consider the supernatural occurrences in the sky that notified wise men of His birth (Matt. 2:1-2) while angels announced it to shepherds nearby (Luke 2:8-14). The news came from above to distinctly different groups – learned, wise men and uneducated shepherds – and it came in ways they would understand. The wise men, likely charting the stars and studying the planets, noticed an anomaly in the sky; the shepherds, outside with their sheep, heard it straight from the angels. This birth was good news of great joy for all people.

Or, it should have been. This news was not well received by those who would reject Jesus as King. Herod the Great, the king of Judea, heard of the birth of this baby boy from the wise men who had traveled from the East. In an attempt to end any potential threat to his throne, Herod had all baby boys in Bethlehem, two years old and under, killed (Matt. 2:16). Joseph was warned of this danger in a dream from God, and his family escaped to Egypt before Jesus was harmed (Matt. 2:13-15). These supernatural events surrounding the ordinary events of Jesus' birth show that while He was a fully human baby, He was no ordinary baby. The miracles that attended His birth announced that His life would be different from all the rest.

A well-known but sometimes misunderstood part of Jesus' life is His birth from the virgin Mary. This supernatural event was predicted in the Old Testament as a sign of the Messiah's birth (Isa. 7:14) and is presented in the New Testament as fact (Luke 1:34, Matt. 1:18-25). That Jesus was conceived by a virgin means there was no sexual union between Mary and a man or Mary and God, but rather this miraculous event was the work of the Holy Spirit, as the Angel described it separately to the unsuspecting Mary (Luke 1:34) and to the surprised Joseph (Matt. 1:20). The same power of God that created the world out of nothing also made God incarnate in the womb of a virgin. Scripture provides no reason for us to think Mary was sinless, although she certainly had a privileged place in redemption history. Scripture speaks directly against claiming she was a perpetual virgin (Matt. 1:25). And there is no scriptural permission given for us to pray to her. So why was Jesus born in this unique manner?

His unique entrance into the world demonstrates that He was not born into sin, as all the rest of Adam's descendants were. Sin entered the world through Adam and that sinful nature was passed down from Father to child. Jesus did not enter the world with an earthly father; rather, His Father was God, showing us that He was born without a sinful nature (Rom. 5:12-32). He was the perfect man, in the perfect sense of the word.

Also significant from the virgin birth is that it signals from the first moment of Jesus' life that His life will be unique from the rest of ours. Jesus was the only man ever to be born of a virgin. Donald Macleod writes of this unique birth, '...[it] is posted on guard at the door of the mystery of Christmas; and none of us must think of hurrying past it. It stands on the threshold of the New Testament, blatantly supernatural, defying our rationalism, informing us that all that follows belongs to the same order as itself and that if we find it offensive there is no point in proceeding further.'[2] Like a warning sign posted outside a rollercoaster cautions the rider before embarking, the miraculous events surrounding Jesus' birth caution us to stop and pay attention to what is about to unfold. Macleod continues, 'If our faith staggers at the virgin birth, what is it going to make of the feeding of the five thousand, the stilling of the tempest, the raising of Lazarus, the transfiguration, the resurrection and, above all, the astonishing self-consciousness of Jesus?'[3]

NORMAL YET UNIQUE

Scripture gives us few details about the childhood of Jesus, although we do know some things. He was the oldest child in a family of at least eight (Matt. 13:55-56), growing up in Nazareth, a small Jewish village of about 400 Aramaic-speaking people. The villagers were probably a few extended families who were mostly farmers and tradesmen. They were Jews living in a world surrounded and dominated by Roman culture. Theirs was an agricultural village with plenty of farmland and open spaces. No doubt the references Jesus made later in His ministry to types of soil, olive trees, and the separation of the wheat from the chaff had their root in His own childhood experiences in the Galilean town. The village was within walking distance to the more ambitious city of Sepphoris, which was being rebuilt to grandeur for most of Jesus' life. Many of the Nazarene craftsmen worked to make this metropolis a significant city that in 4 B.C. Herod Antipas (son of Herod the Great) chose as his capital. Sitting in the shadow of this mighty Roman city was

---

2   Donald Macleod, *The Person of Christ* (Downers Grove, IL: IVP, 1998), p. 37.

3   Ibid.

Nazareth, the irrelevant and backwater town where Jesus was raised. When Phillip told Nathanael the Messiah had been found, his puzzled but honest answer was, 'Can anything good come out of Nazareth?' (John 1:46).

From this insignificant town came a young and humble couple. Mary and Joseph were poor, as evidenced by their offering of a pair of birds at a temple sacrifice after the birth of Jesus when Jewish law called for a lamb (Luke 2:22-24). A provision in the law exempted families in poverty, allowing them to forgo the required sacrifice and offer instead a pair of turtledoves or two young pigeons (Lev. 12:6-8). Astonishingly, the family of the One who created all things did not have enough earthly possessions to make the regular sacrifice at the temple. The One who would be called the Lamb of God – sacrificed on behalf of His people – was born to parents who did not have their own lamb to sacrifice at His birth.

Jesus grew from infancy to a child to a young man. Although His conception was unique, we have no reason to think His early life was outside the bounds of ordinary physical, mental, and emotional development. Jesus grew and matured like any other boy. Luke sums up His childhood with: 'And the child grew and became strong, filled with wisdom. And the favor of God was upon him' (Luke 2:40). While He lived a sinless life, there is no record in Scripture of miracles or of Him acting outside the laws of nature during these years. Scripture only tells us that He grew, both physically and mentally.

Customarily, education of a young Jewish boy in Galilee would begin at home. Mary probably taught her children to chant psalms and some basics of the Hebrew law. Jesus would have learned Jewish history as their community celebrated events like the Passover and would have learned languages as He interacted with them. He spoke Aramaic (the dialect in Nazareth), Greek (the language of the region), and Hebrew (the language of the Scriptures). By age six, Jewish boys were sent to a school known as Bet Sefer, or 'The

House of the Book.' Classes took place at the Synagogue, and Jesus would have studied under the rulers of the synagogues using the Scriptures as a textbook. He would have learned to read (Luke 4:17) and write (John 8:3-9), as He memorized the Torah, which was a goal for all Jewish boys. Mysteriously, the eternal Word of God had to learn God's Word as a boy. Jesus would have studied passages that foretold of a suffering servant and how blood sacrifices were required for sin, but we can only wonder how aware He was as a young boy that He would one day fulfill every prophecy.

Part of Jesus' humanity meant as a child, he had the mind of a child. He was not born in an infant body with the fully developed mind of an adult. Although sinless and still fully God, He thought like a child. He reasoned like a child. He understood like a child. He had to learn to crawl and eat and talk. But Luke tells us He grew and matured. And eventually as He learned Scripture and prayed to God and was guided by the Holy Spirit, He must have at some point come to understand He had a unique relationship with Yahweh. We are not told about the psychological self-awareness of Jesus as a boy, so we must avoid unhealthy speculation. But it is clear that Jesus understood He had a unique relationship with the Father by age twelve. Luke implies this understanding might have been a gradual process as well, as Jesus *grew*, *became*, and *was filled*. His growth, both physically and mentally, was developmental and altogether normal. His coming to understand He was the eternal Son of God, though, would have been completely unique.

While Jesus grew to understand who He was, others did not think of Jesus as anything more than a normal youth. Jesus' own brothers did not believe Him to be the Messiah but thought of Him as a normal kid just like them (John 7:5). These men who lived with Jesus for decades did not recognize Him for who He was until after His resurrection. Even though they never saw Him sin, His brothers did not think Jesus was more than a man. He never lied about His brothers to get them in trouble. Never bullied them.

They never saw Him cheat on His chores. He did not even brag to them about how much Mary loved Him. The brothers must have seen a difference in the life of Jesus, but even so He must have seemed a very normal person. It is easy to imagine as children, the brothers played games with Jesus, saw Him get hurt, laughed with Him, ate meals with Him, saw Him get dirty, learned the carpentry trade with Him, and did normal things normal families do. They saw His humanity up close and therefore did not recognize His divinity, until their eyes were opened to the truth after His death and resurrection. What a remarkable thing for James to eventually say of His earthly brother, 'our Lord Jesus Christ, the Lord of glory' (James 2:1).

At age twelve Jewish boys were considered a 'Son of the Law' and fully responsible for their own actions. By this age, children should have memorized the entire Torah, and most families took their twelve-year-old boys to Jerusalem for their first Passover celebration. In the only narrative recorded in Scripture of His youth, Jesus (in Jerusalem with his family for Passover) showed remarkable understanding of the Scriptures at this age.

Customarily, groups of families from the same community would have traveled together because the journey was several days long and there was safety in numbers from dangers like robbers and wild animals.

After the Passover celebration, the caravan of travelers going back to Nazareth began their journey home, most likely singing the Psalms as they traveled. It seems reasonable to assume the sinless child did not need close parental supervision because it was not until one day into the journey that Mary and Joseph realized Jesus was missing. Three days later, Mary and Joseph eventually found Jesus back in the temple engaging with the rabbis and teachers of the law, astonishing them with His remarkable understanding of the Scriptures. His answer to His befuddled and frustrated parents: 'Why were you looking for me? Did you not know that I must be in my Father's house?' (Luke 2:49). By this point, Jesus surely knew He had a unique relationship with God the Father, and He knew He *must* be about His Father's work. We can only speculate whether Jesus, at this age, understood the symbolism foreshadowed that Passover week or His being found in the temple on the third day. Perhaps Mary and Joseph had chosen this significant age to tell Jesus of His miraculous birth, and He was hungry to learn more from the teachers in the temple. Perhaps He just longed for rich theological discussions that taught Him more about His Father. Perhaps the Passover services in Jerusalem were a watershed moment for young Jesus, as the Holy Spirit deepened His understanding of blood being required to set His people free.

Yet, Jesus left with His parents that day 'and was submissive to them' (Luke 2:51). The One who came to fulfil the law submitted Himself to it fully, obeying and honoring His parents. The Gospel of Luke sums up His teenage years by writing that Jesus 'increased in wisdom and in stature and in favor with God and man' (Luke 2:52). Jesus developed normally from a dependent baby to an obedient boy to a wise young man. Interestingly, Luke notes here the increase of Jesus' favor with God. As the eternal Son of God, the Father's favor with Him cannot increase. But here Luke emphasizes Jesus' humanity. As Jesus grew, remained fully obedient, and increased in His trust for God, He grew in favor with God. In these details of Scripture, we see the ordinariness of Jesus' life; but as any teacher or parent can attest, the details of Jesus' perfect obedience in childhood certainly speak to His uniqueness, as well.

THE CARPENTER

After the temple incident when Jesus was twelve, we know very little about the details of Jesus' life for the next eighteen years. In fact, all we know is summed up in the narrative of His rejection at Nazareth during His ministry. When He began teaching in the synagogue in His hometown where He would have studied as a boy, those present were surprised at the power with which He exposited the Scriptures. They asked, 'Is this not the carpenter?' (Mark 6:3). Surprisingly, the incarnate Son of God's reputation in His own hometown was not as an insightful spiritual leader or eloquent teacher; He was known around town for His skilled labor. The One who created all things by the power of His Word was known primarily for making things with His hands.

For years, Jesus took up Joseph's occupation as a carpenter, learning the trade from His earthly father, as He was made ready for the work of His heavenly Father. Scripture's silence on these eighteen years speaks loudly, as Jesus worked six times longer doing manual labor as a carpenter than He did in public ministry; however, His hidden, laborious, tedious years at a workman's bench were not years spent in vain. The irony was that while He was crafting pieces of wood into useful items for others, He was being made ready to hang on a beam of wood Himself. One hint we have to this fact is found in Hebrews 5:8. 'Although he was a son, he learned obedience through what he suffered. And being made perfect, he became the source of eternal salvation to all who obey him.' Although mysterious, this passage must be speaking to the humanity of Christ, for the emphasis is on *learning*. The divine, all-knowing Son did not have to *learn* anything. But as the man Jesus learned to obey and trust the Father as He was tempted but did not sin, He became the perfect (also translated 'complete'), sinless man. And because of that, He was the perfect substitute for our punishment, the source of eternal salvation. The passage would not make sense if it were arguing that He learned obedience from a singular act of suffering, but rather He learned as He went. With each instance of suffering in His life, with each temptation, He learned to obey the Father. Each small moment of trusting His Father in adversity prepared Him for the next, bigger one until ultimately, He was able to obey the will of the Father, even unto the point of death.

Bruce Ware helps us understand this profound reality when he writes, 'As the Son learned to obey the Father in earlier times of 'lighter' divine demands upon him and consequent 'lighter' suffering – lighter, that is, in comparison both to the divine demands and the suffering he would encounter in the end, as he obeyed the Father in going to the cross – these earlier experiences of faith in the Father's provision, protection, and direction prepared him for the greater acts of obedience he would need to render as he got nearer to the time of the cross.'[4]

You should never undervalue the training in which God may currently have you. You may grow tired of what seems to be insignificant, mundane work. Caring for young children. Housework. Errands. A boring job. Ministry-opportunities that may seem inconsequential. In your temptation to think life is on hold or is going nowhere, remember your faithfulness in the 'small' things God has called you to may be preparing you for faithfulness in 'bigger' things. God may be strengthening your muscles of obedience and faithfulness now in preparation for something that will require greater stamina and fitness. Certainly, God is sanctifying you through your faithfulness in the small acts of obedience He has called you to now.

What 'lighter' suffering did Jesus experience in His life that led to His preparation for the cross? Ware refers to 'the training program necessary to prepare Jesus for the later and much harder obediences that were to come.'[5] We can only speculate what afflictions He experienced in those eighteen years. It seems reasonable to assume His daily suffering was not less than ours, as life was not easy in first century Palestine and Jesus had a much more difficult task in the end to accomplish. Years of manual labor also surely helped prepare His body for the physical challenges of

---

4   Bruce Ware, *The Man Christ Jesus: Theological Reflections on the Humanity of Christ* (Wheaton, IL: Crossway, 2012), p. 64.

5   Ibid.

His public ministry. For the three years detailed in the Gospels, He spent most of His time in active ministry – preaching, teaching, healing, etc. He was with people and traveling for the majority of those years. Calculating only His recorded journeys, He walked over 2,500 miles (over 4,000 km) on foot during that time.[6] He needed a strong physical constitution, and eighteen years of manual labor prepared Him for it.

Jesus clearly experienced the physical limitations of a man. We read in the Scriptures that He got hungry (Mark 11:12, Matt. 21:18) and thirsty (John 19:28) so He ate and drank like any other man. God does not sleep, but Jesus was sometimes tired (John 4:6). He even once slept soundly through a violent storm (Mark 4:38). He was on occasion physically weak. After forty days in the desert, God sent angels to minister to Him (Matt. 4:11). After being bruised and beaten, He was too weak to carry His own cross (Luke 23:26). He looked like a man in every way, and Isaiah even prophesied that He would be a fairly ordinary-looking one (Isa. 53:2). Jesus went so far to affiliate Himself with mankind that He repeatedly called Himself the *Son of Man*, an apocalyptic title, but it was the one He chose to use often, in part to emphasize His humanity.

MAN OF SORROWS

Underscoring Jesus' humanity was the range of human emotions He felt. At times He felt compassion for both individuals and for groups of people (Matt. 14:14, Mark 6:34, Luke 7:13). Jesus described Himself as being 'sorrowful, even to death' while praying in the Garden of Gethsemane (Matt. 26:38). Hours before that, His soul was troubled (John 12:27; 13:21). Hebrews describes Jesus as offering up 'prayers and supplications, with loud cries and tears' (Heb. 5:7). During His ministry, He experienced both anger (Matt. 21:12-13, Mark 11:15-18, John 2:13-22) and joy (John 15:11, Luke 10:21, John 17:13).

---

6   J. Oswald Sanders, *The Incomparable Christ* (Chicago, IL: Moody Publishers, 2009), p. 71.

In the shortest verse in the Bible, we learn He knew grief as He mourned the death of His good friend Larazus (John 11:35).

After visiting with Lazarus' two grieving sisters Martha and Mary, *Jesus wept*. He saw His friends experiencing the grief of death and was 'moved in his spirit and greatly troubled' (John 11:33). Perhaps Jesus cried because He had such compassion for those who were suffering, or perhaps He wept because He was grieving over sin and its consequences. Whatever the cause of His tears, Jesus was moved deeply and emotionally. He did not merely wipe a tear from His eye and blame it on those awful Judean allergies this time of year. He unashamedly *wept* outside of Lazarus' tomb.

Perhaps the strongest and most obvious emotion Jesus felt was that of love (John 15:9-17, Rom. 5:8, Rom. 8:37-39). We know 'Jesus loved Martha and her sister and Lazarus' (John 11:5). John refers to himself as 'the disciple whom Jesus loved' (John 13:23). Jesus refers to His own love for His disciples and commands them to use that love as a template for how to love others. 'A new commandment I give you, that you love one another: just as I have loved you, you also are to love one another. By this all people will know that you are my disciples, if you have love for one another' (John 13:34-35). Love motivated Jesus to serve and eventually die for His people. In one particularly moving story, a wealthy young man saw Jesus and pleaded with Him for the knowledge of how to obtain eternal life. This young ruler explained to Jesus that he had kept the laws of God since childhood, but Jesus knew of this man's great affection for his money. So Jesus told the young man to sell all of his possessions and follow Him. Jesus could have harshly rebuked this wealthy ruler, but instead 'Jesus 'looked at him and loved him' (Mark 10:21, NIV).

This same love demonstrated by Jesus was how the Old Testament described God's love for His people. It was often referred to as 'steadfast' (Deut.7:9, Ps. 86:15, Ps. 136:26). Love for the world led God to send Jesus to rescue sinners (John 3:16). And it wasn't just a vague love for the world in general but love for real people – one that motivated him 'to give himself for me' (Gal. 2:20), as Paul said. This love demonstrated by God provides the motivation and instruction in how we are to love one another (1 John 4:9-11).

Jesus had a fully human emotional experience. John Calvin once helpfully said, 'Christ has put on our feelings along with our flesh.' And yet, uniquely, His emotions never led Him to sin. There are some emotions that Jesus never felt. Jesus never experienced fear, anxiety, worry, self-pity, or an unrighteous hatred or anger. We get angry and lash out. We feel sad and wallow in self-pity. But Jesus was never controlled by His emotions nor did He use His emotions to manipulate others. He did not stuff His emotions away, He was not embarrassed by them, and He did not elevate them beyond their proper place. In Christ, we see the purity of emotions as God intended them, not a sinful misuse of them. We see one who is fully human like us, and yet unique from us.

TEMPTATION

Hebrews beautifully instructs us that we have a high priest who can 'sympathize with our weaknesses, but one who in every respect has been tempted as we are, yet without sin' (Heb. 4:15). Jesus is able to sympathize with our weaknesses because He fully knows the limitations of man. He does not know our weaknesses from afar, but He is intimately acquainted with our frailty. In fact, He understands our weaknesses better than any man on earth because He has experienced the fullness of temptation and never succumbed to it. He knows better than we do the full breadth and depth of how powerful temptation to sin is. Sins that we quickly succumb to, Jesus resisted His entire life. In His humanity, Christ faced real temptation toward real sin.

While Jesus was born without a sinful nature, He faced a barrage of temptation to sin unlike any other man on the planet. Satan used all the tools at his disposal to bring down the perfect Son of God, tempting Him among other things toward power, a painless victory, and idolatry. Satan surely brought a relentless, heightened, unending assault of schemes intended to entrap the Messiah and thwart God's plan for forgiveness.

Yet Jesus never gave in to the temptation. He never sinned in public or private. He never told a half-truth, never gossiped, never lost His temper in anger. He never gave in or up in that fight against sin, relentless as it may have been. He fought every time and fought until He was victorious. The temptations must have only grown more intense as He neared death, as He became increasingly aware of the agony He would undergo. The temptation to abort the mission was so great by the time He reached the Garden of Gethsemane, He literally began to sweat blood. He pleaded with His closest companions on earth to stay awake to pray for Him. While He faced the full barrage of temptation to refuse His Father's will, His disciples quickly and easily gave in to the desire to sleep.

Because Jesus knows all our temptations yet remained sinless we can 'with confidence draw near to the throne of grace that we may receive mercy and find grace to help in time of need' (Heb. 4:15-16). We plead for help in fighting sin at the throne of grace, where we find Jesus, the God-man who understands our pleas. He is not a far-away deity, unaware of the temptations we face. We go to Him confidently because He is sympathetic in our time of need. He understands the struggles humans face, because He lived a fully human existence. We go to Him also because He was without sin. He knows how to resist temptation. And He serves as the perfect high priest on our behalf. At His throne we don't find condemnation or fear. There, He distributes grace and mercy to His beloved children. He is ruling from that throne, but He does so understanding the trials of living in this fallen world.

Jesus was the perfect man. He lived a perfect life. But He didn't only take on flesh to live, He came to die.

Jesus Died and Rose Again

The ultimate proof that Jesus was fully human was His death on a cross. As a human being with flesh and blood, Jesus experienced a physical death – and one that was excruciatingly painful. Islam teaches God supernaturally removed Jesus from the cross, so He would not experience the painful death of crucifixion, but the Bible tells us the opposite to be true. Jesus experienced the physical, emotional, and spiritual torment of death on a cross.

Crucifixion was invented by the Persians several hundred years before Jesus' death, and the Romans reserved this form of capital punishment for the vilest criminals. The Romans utilized several options for crucifixion (arms straight above head, arms tied out to the side, or arms nailed to a horizontal wooden beam), causing varying degrees of pain and prolonging of death. As in Jesus' case, the victims were often flogged with a whip before their crucifixion so that gouges of ripped skin were exposed across their backs. The resulting pain was severe punishment in itself, but it was only the beginning of the physical torment for one sentenced to death on a cross. Jesus' flogging left Him too weak to carry the thirty-pound wooden beam of His cross to the place of crucifixion as was customary, so soldiers forced Simon from Cyrene to carry it for Him (Mark 15:21, Luke 23:26).

To attach someone to a cross, soldiers would bend the victim's knees at a forty-five-degree angle and drive nails through his feet or heels. Because of the distribution of the victim's weight on the cross, breathing was laborious and difficult. In order to breathe while upright on the wooden cross, victims had to push up with their legs, putting their entire weight on the nails in their feet. Each breath then caused the nail holes in their feet to grow wider. With each push of their legs to gasp for breath, the victims' bodies would move up and down the rough, vertical, wooden beam, and the open wounds on their backs from the flogging would rip even more. Often after hours of this excruciatingly painful and slow death, executioners would break the victims' legs in order to speed up the death process. The Gospel of John records the Roman soldiers breaking the legs of the two criminals crucified with Jesus so that the men would die and their bodies could be removed from their crosses before the Sabbath (John 19:31-33). Once the legs were broken or gave way from exhaustion, the victims would rely on their outstretched arms for strength to pull them up in order to breathe.

Death usually took longer for victims who were tied to a cross. If the victims were nailed to a cross, long nails were driven through their palms or wrists so these smaller bones could eventually support their body weight. This wound alone caused immense pain as it severed the median nerve. As the heaviness of the victim's body strained the outstretched arms, the shoulders eventually were pulled from their sockets, followed by elbows, and then wrists. In time, the arms were of no use to help the victims breathe, and death by suffocation usually ensued. If suffocation was not imminent, death likely would occur because a lack of oxygen in the bloodstream led to failing organs or built-up fluid in the lungs or the heart.

This form of capital punishment was intentionally performed outside the city walls but in public to shame the victim and to deter would-be criminals from wayward behavior. It was a brutal way to die that deliberately involved immense physical pain, as well as emotional torment. As Jesus suffered physically, those who opposed Him callously watched His pain and mocked Him in His agony. They made fun of His claim to be divine and that He called Himself 'king.' How ironic, the 'king of the Jews' hanging helplessly on a cross. He saw His family and friends watching in horror, and He knew they were both shocked and frightened at what was happening. And yet Jesus could not comfort them. He must have felt great anguish at watching their grief, unable to explain to them what was happening or help them in their distress.

As torturous as Jesus' death was on many levels, it was not unique. Romans crucified other men they believed to be criminals. Two others died the same day Jesus did. Roman citizens, however, were exempt from this type of corporal punishment; it was a death so heinous in nature that it was reserved strictly for foreigners. Take in that thought. The One for whom, by whom, and through whom this world was created allowed Himself to be treated as a foreigner in His own creation and suffered one of the most agonizing deaths possible at the hands of His own creatures. John Wesley pondered it and wrote of his astonishment: 'Tis mystery all, the immortal dies.'[7]

In modern times, we try to make sure our own deaths are as painless as possible. We hope we might die peacefully in our sleep or with enough morphine to numb our sense of pain. Or perhaps we refuse to even think about death for fear of the suffering that may be involved. We do not like to linger long on what it must have been like for Jesus to feel every wooden splinter in His fleshless back, or to think of every breath for hours being laboriously difficult and painful.

Historical references unanimously agree that Jesus was killed on a Friday, and the following Sunday morning His body was missing from the grave. Scripture is clear that He was raised from the dead on the third day, according to what He (and the rest of the Scriptures) had predicted (John 2:18-22, Matt. 12:39-40).

Jesus, the God-man for Eternity

Over the next forty days as the resurrected Jesus was on earth, He appeared to hundreds of people, leaving many eyewitnesses to His resurrection. In the details of these encounters, evidence shows His resurrected body was still a real human body. (Matt. 28:9, Luke 24:30-31, 24:39-43). So normal looking was He that many mistook His appearance for that of an ordinary stranger. Even the

---

7   Lyrics from 'And Can It Be', Charles Wesley, 1738.

disciples did not recognize Jesus when He appeared among them (Luke 24:31, 37).

But in one of the most extraordinary aspects of the incarnation, His physical, human body did not disappear at the end of those forty days. In front of His apostles on the Mount of Olives, Jesus ascended into heaven *in His human body*. The angels who accompanied Him as He rose into the heavens said to the apostles who witnessed this miraculous event, 'This Jesus, who was taken up from you into heaven, will come in the same way as you saw him go into heaven' (Acts 1:11). Jesus retained His humanity as He left earth for heaven, and the angels promised that He will return in His human body as well. The eternal Son of God became incarnate, not in a temporary state but an eternal one. Jesus did not put on a human costume for the brief season He was on earth. When He became the Son of Man, He put on a whole new aspect to His being forever. He *became* one of us for the rest of eternity. Even right now, Jesus is awaiting His return to earth for the second time in His physical, resurrected body. He has elbows and fingernails and scars in His hands and feet, as He waits to gather His people in their own resurrected bodies for eternity.

Questions

Fully Man

The incarnate Jesus took on full humanity when He came to earth as a baby. He displayed His humanity in His growth, maturity, development, emotions, and His physical death. He was fully man, and yet He was a unique man. He was not born into sin and He never sinned. After His death, He was resurrected from the grave and returned to heaven – this time in a new, glorified body that He will retain forever.

1. How can Jesus' humanity bring Noura (p. 85) comfort?

2. In order to grasp what it means that Jesus was a man, we first need to understand what it means to be human. Throughout history, there have been many different views on how to define humankind apart from the rest of creation (i.e. Aristotle said humans were unique because we have the ability to reason, evolutionary scientists argue we are uniquely human because we fit into a unique nomenclature). But the best place to start with defining mankind is of course with man's Creator. Read Genesis 1:26-31. What can we learn about God's intention for mankind (before the fall) from these verses? What work did God give man to do? What direction did He give them? In whose image did He make them?

3. English poet Alexander Pope made famous the line, 'To err is human.' Why is this statement false in light of how human beings were created by God? How does Jesus show us this is false?

4. Our first father Adam was the original head of the human race – the original 'son of God' – but he failed to live up to his expectations in this role. How did he fall short of what he was created to do?

5. Jesus was a fully human baby boy but supernatural events surrounded Him from the beginning. What are some of the things being signaled to the world about this baby right from the very beginning of His life?

6. While we do not have a lot of details about Jesus' childhood recorded in Scripture, we have no reason to think His early life was outside the bounds of ordinary physical, mental, and emotional development. Read these passages and write down what you see that speaks to Jesus' physical life: Mark 11:12, John 19:28, John 4:6.

7. Jesus felt a range of different human emotions (Matt. 9:36, Isa. 53:3, Matt. 26:38, John 12:27, John 15:11, Heb. 5:7, John 11:35). Yet, the most obvious and important emotion Jesus felt was that of love. Read Galatians 2:20. Who is the beneficiary of this love? What are we to do in light of that? Read 1 John 4: 9-11.

8. While it was always miraculous, other people besides Jesus had been raised from the dead (Jairus' daughter and Lazarus are two of them). Jesus experienced a truly unique beginning and ending to His earthly life. What was unique about His birth and what was unique about His resurrection from the dead?

9. Read Acts 1:10-11. What do the angels say to the apostles about Jesus? What does this tell us about the physical body of Jesus? What is the significance of the ascension? Why is it important that the risen (and still human) Jesus went back into heaven? If Jesus still has an earthly body, even now, what does that say about His continued ministry for us in heaven?

10. After the resurrection, Thomas touched the scars Jesus had from the cross (John 20:24-29). What purpose would God have in not healing these scars in Jesus' resurrected body? Why is it significant that He bear those scars eternally?

Chapter 5

Made Like His Brothers

Jada's adult son has been wayward for years. Trapped by addiction and plagued by bad choices, he has been in and out of jail and rehab facilities for most of his adult life. Jada is ready to give up. She believes the light of hope for her son has grown so dim she can no longer see it. He is doomed to failure, she says. Sure, she has seen God help a lot of people, but her son is in too deep. She wants to hold onto hope, but she is done with clever quotes and pithy sayings that hold no real hope for change. As she describes her pain, you realize she needs something weighty and real to hold onto. How can you help Julia?

As a mother of five young children, it is not unusual for complete strangers to ask about my family. The question I hear most often at the grocery store or the playground is, 'Are they all yours?' The most awkward question I hear is, 'Do you not believe in birth control?' The most surprising question came one spring afternoon when my children and some of their entrepreneurial friends set up a lemonade stand in front of our house. Someone stopped their car to ask me the name of our school. I took that as a compliment. They could have asked, 'What is the name of your circus?'

One of the sweetest questions I often hear is, 'Who does he/she look like?' It is an obvious question when we see a child. We look to see whom they resemble. Children inherit physical features from their parents, but parents also pass on things like habits and genetic medical history. We look to the older generation to see things we want to imitate or avoid as we get older. This is natural. Watching our parents gives us a foreshadowing of what life may be like down the road.

God also raised up men in history whose lives help us better understand Jesus: human figures given to foreshadow His life and help us to understand more clearly His work. They tell us things about the person and the work of Jesus, and they do so in a 3-dimensional, understandable kind of way. Hebrews writes 'he had to be made like his brothers in every respect, so that he might become a merciful and faithful high priest in the service of God, to make propitiation for the sins of the people. For because he himself has suffered when tempted, he is able to help those who are being tempted' (Heb. 2:17-18). Because Jesus was made like us in every way, He is able to provide salvation and help in our times of need. This chapter is intended to observe the lives of some of the men who served as early 'types' of Christ, those who pre-figured Him to help us better know Him.

As we have already considered in part, Adam was one of these men – so was King David and the High Priests of the Old Testament. Jesus became the Second Adam, the perfect Davidic King, the Great High Priest, and He is now ruling and actively working for our good as the God-man in heaven.

A New Adam: Our New Leader

THE FIRST MAN

Innocence and life that were present everywhere in Genesis 1-2 were suddenly replaced by guilt and death in Genesis 3 when Adam succumbed to the temptation to move beyond the good boundaries he had been given by God. Not realizing that they already resembled their God because they had been created in His image (and at the time still sinless), Adam and Eve jumped at the opportunity presented to them by the serpent to be 'like God.' This wasn't simply a blunder or a misstep. This was an act of treason as God's creatures sought to seize God's authority instead of living under it. And in doing so, they fundamentally undermined what it means to be a son of God.

This first sin introduced death into God's perfect world, just as God promised (Gen. 2:17). It set into motion a darker world and a distorted nature for mankind. From that point forward, spiritual and physical death would now be the twin towers that would loom over every culture and nation in what was once a perfect world.

Adam as the first man on earth served as the representative of the whole human race. In choosing disobedience and rebellion, he broke the perfect communion that existed between God and man; and, as a representative figure, he did so on behalf of all mankind. In the garden, we as the human race fell from our elevated state of innocence and intimacy with God and plunged into sin. While we retain the image of God, that image is now stained by the sin that has touched every part of our humanity. We are now strange creatures who still bear the image but do so in a way that is tarnished and scarred.

THE SECOND MAN

Because the first man failed at his task to truly be human, the Bible speaks of the need for a 'Last Adam' or 'Second Man' (1 Cor. 15:45-57). Jesus is that Second Man. He is the Last Adam. Their similarities are many: they both had miraculous beginnings, being specially created by God Himself. Both were created innocent, perfect, and without original sin, the only two humans ever born outside the bondage to sin. Both served as representatives of humanity. Both were rulers who were given dominion over creation. And, in both, a deep sleep produced a beautiful bride. (Through Adam's sleep, God opened his side and created Eve; through Jesus' death, blood and water poured out of His side, and His beloved bride, the church, was born.) Both Adam and Jesus were tested, but one disobeyed while the other obeyed. Adam's disobedience brought death and curse on all of humanity. Jesus' obedience brought life and righteousness for all who believe. One obeyed the serpent; the other crushed his head.

These similarities are not mere coincidences. Jesus came to earth as a human to accomplish what Adam failed to do. As the two representatives of the human race they are like two kings, and we are all subjects under one of them. We can live under the reign of Adam or we can live under the reign of Christ. In Adam, we are born spiritually dead under the power of sin that leads to physical death. In Christ, we are born again to a new life that will last for eternity. All those who are living under the reign of Adam have the opportunity to transfer kingdoms because Christ's free gift of salvation is bigger than Adam's transgression. Paul explained this concept to the Romans: '... as one trespass led to condemnation for all men, so one act of righteousness leads to justification and life for all men.' (Rom. 5:18). We already know death through Adam, but now we can know life through Jesus.

In order for Jesus to represent a new humanity that would no longer be under the reign of Adam, His life had to be set apart in a different way. The human race needed a redeemer, but we could not produce this representative ourselves. As advanced and civilized as we like to pride ourselves on being, human beings could not manufacture salvation on our own or even from one of our own. No advances in education, technology, or philosophy could produce what we needed most. Mankind's redeemer had to come from outside of us to rescue us.

The promised One entered the world to reboot humanity. We needed a new beginning, not just a reawakening or a better example for living. The human condition post-fall is so dire that a supernatural eruption into the plight of man was necessary. Unlike all the sons of Adam, Jesus was born different – He was born innocent. Born of a virgin. Adam was not His father. He stands on His own.

Jesus' entrance onto the stage of human history over 2,000 years ago had massive consequences for the human race. No longer does humanity have to be consigned to graveyards and death. In Jesus, life has come into this world and destroyed death's sting. In Jesus, a new path has been secured. By faith in the Last Adam – human beings can regain the glorious destiny that we forfeited in that garden of innocence at the very beginning.

Jesus restores the image of God in man. In 1 Corinthians, Paul writes, 'Just as we have borne the image of the man of dust, we shall also bear the image of the man of heaven' (1 Cor. 15:49). Paul writes at times as if the only people on earth who matter are Adam and Jesus. They represent everyone else who has lived, and they do so in stark contrast to one another. Each person on earth will be loyal to one side or the other. In the language of the iGeneration, we will be either #TeamAdam or #TeamJesus and which side we are determines whose image we bear and where we will spend eternity.

A New People

As the Last Adam, Jesus became the head of a new group of people. Before Jesus, God's covenant people were the ethnic Israelites. God chose to reveal His law to them, and as they obeyed it, they would live distinctly from the rest of the world. God's desire was to bless the world as the Gentile nations watched the pattern set by the Israelites living by faith in submission to Him, the one true God. But, like the first Adam, the Jewish people failed to trust God. And they rejected Jesus as their head. So Jesus spoke these fateful words to their leaders, 'Therefore I tell you, the kingdom of God will be taken away from you and given to a people producing its fruits' (Matt. 21:43).

Through His life, death, resurrection, and ascension, Jesus created a new people, a new assembly. The church is God's people who have been drawn together under the headship of the Lord Jesus Christ. Now – through this group of people – God is producing fruit for His kingdom. The universal church, made up of the people who trust in Jesus as savior, are now both Gentiles and Jews. Africans, Americans, Arabs, Asians, Australians – all manner of ethnic, linguistic, and socio-economic status are included in the people of God. Those who are in Christ are the new Israel. We are the chosen people of God who are to live distinct lives from the rest of the world and are to bless all the nations of the world through the knowledge of the one, true God. I am a member of a local church with people from nearly 30 different nations. We are a diverse group of people in most every way. Our native languages are different. Our skin and hair colors vary. Our clothing styles are noticeably different. We are maids, construction workers, teachers, and CEOs of companies. Some of us are highly educated, and some of us never finished high school. On the surface, we have very little in common. But we are all united under the headship of Christ. We are a small representation of the universal body of Christ, this new race of people called into Christ's kingdom by grace.

If you are in Christ, you are part of something bigger than yourself. You are part of a corporate group of people who are chosen by God to be His beloved people. Your destiny is tied up with that of your head, the Lord Jesus Christ. Your significance is found in Him. This group identity is more defining of you than your ethnic background, country of origin, or career. God is weaving a beautifully diverse tapestry of people from all tribes, tongues, and nations, and if you are in Christ, you are part of that exquisite fabric.

Those who are in Christ have been transferred into a new spiritual realm with a new spiritual status. To this world, your importance changes based on things like money, power, and fame. I used to be Chief of Staff for a U.S. Senator, and my importance to many people was directly connected to the power I had access to. I participated in meetings with high-ranking officials and was invited to elite events. I even attended meetings at the White House, occasionally with the President of the United States. After I left my job to be a stay at home mom, I did not get any more invitations from the White House. I traded in my suits for buttoning on a baby carrier. Not only did my wardrobe change dramatically, my job (and my status) had changed. In Christ, we have reached a status far more elite than we can even imagine. It is more prestigious than anything this world offers. It will not be unveiled to the world until the last day, but for now we are safely hidden away in Christ. Under Christ, we are part of a whole new race of people with unimaginable access and privileges – access and privilege that can never be taken away. We have direct access to the God of the universe, the One who holds the hearts of earthly kings in His hands (Prov. 21:1). We are privileged to be a part of God's grand plans for the world. We know and experience a freedom from sin that those in bondage to the ways of the world will never know. We are part of a whole new privileged class people with Christ as our head.

A New David: Our New King

Another picture God provided to foreshadow – and thus better understand – the Lord Jesus, comes through King David, the great King of Israel. Matthew's gospel begins, 'The book of the genealogy of Jesus Christ, the son of David, the son of Abraham' (Matt. 1:1).

Matthew immediately wants his readers to see the connection between David and Jesus – that Jesus is the promised Son of David. Years earlier God had told David that He would raise up an offspring whose kingdom would last forever, 'Your house and your kingdom shall be made sure forever before me. Your throne shall be established forever' (2 Sam. 7:16). Matthew wants his readers to see that the son promised to David had come to be king.

Similar to the list of comparisons between Adam and Jesus, the parallels between King David and Jesus are easily identified. David was a shepherd boy who became the Jewish King. Jesus, called King of the Jews, was the Shepherd who was tasked with leading God's people. Both David and Jesus had meager and humble beginnings in life. Both began to usher in their kingdoms at age 30. Both fearlessly defeated impossible foes: David, as a boy, slayed a man who was at least twice his size; Jesus defeated our greatest enemy – sin and death. Both rose to their positions because the one before them failed. Both David and Jesus faced fierce opposition and were betrayed by friends. Both showed remarkable kindness to the helpless and even former foes. Is there a more beautiful analogy of our salvation in Scripture than that displayed by the powerful King David inviting the son of his former rival, the lame Mephibosheth, to eat at his table for the rest of his days 'like one of the King's sons'? (2 Sam. 9). The communion table is where former enemies of Jesus now gather, but we will one day feast at King Jesus' table with Him forever (Luke 14:15; 22:30). Scripture says the Holy Spirit carried them both along while they both spoke the words of God (2 Sam. 23:2, 2 Pet. 1:21, Luke 4:1). David convinced God to withhold judgment from the Israelite people, and even offered to be the substitute for the people (2 Sam. 24:17-25). Jesus took all the judgment for His people, and God accepted His offer to be the substitute for them. David provided the materials needed to build a temple to house the sanctuary of God; Jesus Himself was the temple of God that was torn down and rebuilt in three days. David bought land for the altar of God on Gentile ground; Christ offered the sacrifice of Himself to the Gentiles. God promised David someone from his lineage would sit on the throne forever; Jesus is the forever king from the line of David who would rule the world.

CREATOR TO KING

Psalm 2 foreshadows what God would give to the future, faithful Davidic King: 'Ask of me, and I will make the nations your heritage, and the ends of the earth your possession' (Ps. 2:8). This Psalm promised an *inheritance* of nations and the earth as Christ's eventual possession. By definition, your inheritance is something that is at one point not in your possession. It is something given to you. There is an expectation you will receive it at a time in the future. In his letter to the Ephesians, Paul described the inheritance Jesus received post-resurrection: God the Father 'raised him from the dead and [then] seated him at his right hand in the heavenly places, far above all rule and authority and power and dominion, and above every name that is named, not only in this age but also in the one to come. And he put all things under his feet and gave him as head over all things to the church...' (Eph. 1:20-23). God the Father inaugurated Jesus as head and ruler over all things as He raised Him from the dead (Rom. 1:4).

Did Steve Jobs have to go to the Apple Store to buy an iPhone? Does Vera Wang have to purchase one of her own wedding dresses? Does an artist go to an auction and bid on her own work? We know from Scripture that everything in creation was made by and for the beloved Son of God (Col. 1:15-16, John 1:1-4, Heb. 1:1- 2) – from Him, through Him, and to Him. As Creator of all things and the One for whom all things were made, He certainly has a divine right to all things. But Scripture seems to signal a shift in cosmic responsibilities given to Jesus after His resurrection. He went from Creator to King. How do we make sense of how the Creator of all things has somehow earned the right to rule over His own creation?

Paul explains that Jesus' obedience and humility earned Him the exalted status of king and ruler of all: 'And being found in human form, he humbled himself by becoming obedient to the point of death, even death on a cross. *Therefore* God has highly exalted him and bestowed on him the name that is above every name...' (Phil. 2:8-9, emphasis mine). Because of Jesus' perfect obedience and conformity to the Father's will, even to the point of an unspeakably painful death, the Father has exalted Jesus and granted to Him all authority and dominion. The Father has put all things under His feet, and Jesus is now 'at the right hand of God, with angels, authorities, and powers under his rule' (1 Pet. 3:22). This reign is over all the earth, all nations, and all people.

What Jesus did on earth in the flesh mattered eternally. This new exaltation, dominion, and rule is given to the One who perfectly fulfilled all He was sent to do. Jesus' shift in cosmic responsibilities makes sense when we understand they are granted now to the God-man Jesus Christ. Bruce Ware writes, 'Such "newness" has no appropriate "fit" with the deity of Christ, but it surely does with this human Son, this Messiah, this son of David, who is granted as his reward the rulership of the world he has won and conquered.'[1] King David conquered His enemies and won the right to rule over Israel. Jesus, the God-man, conquered His enemies through obedience to the Father and therefore earned the right to be king. He was the sinless one in the line of King David prophesied in Psalm 2 to be given the nations as His heritage and the ends of the earth as His possession.

At the cross Jesus won this earthly domain back from Satan. God still retained ultimate sovereignty over His creation, but Satan had taken on a new role post-fall. When God withdrew His presence from the garden after the fall, room was left for Satan and his minions to prowl the earth on a long leash and with some measure of authority (Eph. 2:1-3).

---

1   Ware, *The Man Christ Jesus*, pp. 133-134.

When Satan tempted Jesus for 40 days in the wilderness, he offered to delegate some of his rule to Jesus: 'To you I will give all this authority and their glory, for it has been delivered to me, and I give it to whom I will. If you, then, will worship me, it will all be yours' (Luke 4:6-7). Jesus' response to the devil was simply, 'It is written, "You shall worship the Lord your God, and him only shall you serve"' (Luke 4:8). Jesus did not call into question whether Satan had authority over the nations; rather, Jesus flatly refused the devil's offer of an easier way to win them back than the path laid before Him by His Father. Jesus took the painful road of the cross and crushed Satan under His foot, taking back the kingdom for eternity.

In light of this reality, consider the glory of Jesus' words to His disciples before He ascended into heaven. 'All authority in heaven and on earth has been given to me. Go therefore and make disciples of all nations, baptizing them in the name of the Father and of the Son and of the Holy Spirit, teaching them to observe all that I have commanded you' (Matt. 28:18-20). As the God-man, King Jesus has defeated Satan and won back authority over the nations, and with His authority He commissioned His followers to go and make disciples. Jesus' disciples go out under the authority of the King of Kings to gather His people home.

Satan no longer reigns. He continues to rage, but he does not have the authority he once had to reign. He has not been totally destroyed, of course. That final defeat of the serpent will not happen until Christ's second coming. But he has been bound from having any authority over the church. He can tempt, he can attack, he can throw darts, but he will not overcome. This truth gives the Christian a real confidence in God. Anxiety over the headlines is replaced with trust that God is in control. Fear about the future is calmed with knowledge that evil does not reign. Try as it might, the world and the devil simply cannot triumph over King Jesus on His throne.

NATIONS, BE WARNED

My friend Rebecca is an expert analyst on nuclear deterrence. If you live in the United States, you may have seen her on the news talking about the worldwide threat that stems from North Korea gaining nuclear capabilities. She recently relayed a conversation she had with a member of Congress as she was briefing him on how advanced North Korea's nuclear missile program had become. The bewildered Congressman asked her how she knew so much classified information about the threat without seeming panicked. Her response was simply that they should act with diligence to mitigate the threat from North Korea, but her confidence was (thankfully) not in the US government. Rather, it was in God alone. He has final control over all things. This is what it means to live confidently in Christ. We work to make the world a better place, confident that Jesus is on the true throne of the universe. We trust God is the final judge and sovereign ruler over all things.

Consider again Psalm 2, which prophesies King Jesus' rule over the nations.

I will tell of the decree:
The LORD said to me, 'You are my Son;
    today I have begotten you.
Ask of me, and I will make the nations your heritage,
    and the ends of the earth your possession.
You shall break them with a rod of iron
    and dash them in pieces like a potter's vessel.'
Now therefore, O kings, be wise;
    be warned, O rulers of the earth.
Serve the LORD with fear,
    and rejoice with trembling.
Kiss the Son,
    lest he be angry, and you perish in the way,
    for his wrath is quickly kindled.
Blessed are all who take refuge in him.

Nations, be warned and take refuge in Jesus. Despite being ignored by the nightly news and considered irrelevant by this world, the risen Jesus will judge the nations, calling even the most powerful rulers to account. King Jesus has earned the right to rule over all the nations of this earth.

Recently, I sat with a friend who told me of her father's murder in a village raid in Sudan when she was only six years old. Shortly after that, I read several accounts of Myanmar soldiers systematically killing men, raping women, and burning babies in a Rohingya village in Southeast Bangladesh. My anger toward such despicable acts raged as I imagined the nightmare many of these defenseless women faced and the deep sorrow they will face for the rest of their lives as they mourn the loss of their loved ones and attempt to heal from their tragically broken lives. The only comfort I find in light of these true horror stories is the knowledge that the King of the universe does not watch defenselessly or passively in situations of wickedness and injustice.

Revelation 19 describes the day of judgment in a vivid way as the birds of the air are invited to gorge on the flesh of the wicked of this world after their eternal defeat. Jesus is described as having a 'sharp sword with which to strike down the nations, and he will rule them with a rod of iron' (Rev. 19:15). King Jesus will defeat His enemies easily. The One who is called 'Faithful and True,' 'The Word of God,' 'King of kings,' and 'Lord of lords' will set all things right in His universe. If you are someone who has been treated wickedly or unjustly in this world, be encouraged by these words. It was prophesied long ago and will soon come to pass—the wicked will be brought to justice by King Jesus.

A New High Priest: Our Final Sacrifice

Maybe your biggest struggle is not someone's wicked actions toward you, but rather the injustice you have done to another. Perhaps you are racked with guilt about sexual sin or a broken relationship or feeling you have let God down. I recently read a letter from a distraught and grieving woman who asked, 'What would you say to a Christian who had an abortion and struggles to believe God loves her?' This woman knows all too well that Jesus will one day judge wickedness; she needs to hear words of comfort for God's people.

The amazing news is that there are words of comfort for her. Take heart! We have a 'great high priest.' Hebrews says, 'Since then we have a great high priest who has passed through the heavens, Jesus, the Son of God, let us hold fast our confession. For we do not have a high priest who is unable to sympathize with our weaknesses, but one who in every respect has been tempted as we are, yet without sin. Let us then with confidence draw near to the throne of grace, that we may receive mercy and find grace to help in time of need' (Heb. 4:14-16).

Not by the Blood of Goats

Under the Old Testament law, God required a sacrifice for atonement to forgive sin. These sacrifices were almost always of an unblemished animal, and a priest was required to perform the duty of the sacrifice. It was not a private individual act between a person and God; rather, the priest had to go between the offender and God. He was a mediator. In addition to specific sacrifices made throughout the year, one particular day every year was set aside by God as a special day to purge the people and the temple from defilement. This Day of Atonement was immensely important to the Jewish community, with God requiring a fast from all the people. On that day (and only that day), the high priest would enter the Holy of Holies – where God Himself dwelt – to offer the sacrifice that would atone for the sins of the people. Given this yearly ritual and all the daily sacrifices made by the priests for the sins of the people, the Jewish community understood deeply that blood sacrifice was necessary for the forgiveness of their sins.

When the writer of Hebrews refers to Jesus as our great high priest, the meaning is unmistakable. He is the mediator between man and God, the One who is able to make atonement on behalf of His people. He is the One who entered the Holy of Holies, giving His own life as a sacrifice, not one day a year, but once for all, now dwelling there before the Father for eternity. While the high priests under the old covenant had to make atonement for their own sin and then repeat their sacrifices over and over, Jesus had no sin. His sacrifice was sufficient for all His people for all time. 'He entered once for all into the holy places, not by means of the blood of goats and calves but by means of his own blood, thus securing an eternal redemption' (Heb. 9:12). He is the only possible eternal mediator between a holy God and sinful man, and He does not require the blood sacrifice of an unblemished animal. He is that eternal mediator by His own blood.

No Condemnation Here

The Christian life should be one filled with sobriety about sin but joy over its defeat. May our anthem be, 'There is now no condemnation for those who are in Christ Jesus' (Rom. 8:1). If you are in Christ, your sin, no matter how large and seemingly unforgivable, has been atoned for by our great high priest, who lives to intercede for you before the holy God. To the Christian woman who had an abortion and is struggling to believe God loves her: confidently approach the throne of grace, where you will find mercy deeper than you can imagine.

Some of us struggle with sins of our past that haunt us and seem unforgivable. Others of us struggle in a seemingly slow climb up the mountain of sanctification. We grow weary and are easily discouraged by the constant bombardment of temptation and how often we find ourselves giving into it. Consider what John writes in 1 John, 'My little children, I am writing this to you so that you may not sin. But if anyone does sin, we have an advocate with the Father, Jesus Christ the righteous. He is the propitiation for our sins, and not only for ours but also for the sins of the whole world' (1 John. 2:1-2).

While Jesus is seated at the right hand of the Father in heaven, serving as our great high priest and reigning over the world, He is our personal advocate with the Father. We cannot possibly know all that these verses mean in terms of Christ's advocacy for us, but we can know with certainty that it means good news for sinners–that we will never be turned away.

In preaching from 1 John, John Piper said, '…Christ is our attorney and his portfolio is his propitiation. He stands before his Father in heaven, and every time we sin, he doesn't make a new propitiation. He doesn't die again and again. Instead he opens his portfolio and lays the exhibits of Good Friday on the bench before the Judge. Photographs of the crown of thorns, the lashing, the mocking soldiers, the agonies of the cross, and the final cry of victory: It is finished.'[2] While we may at times grow weary of our own sin, Jesus never grows weary. There is no maximum amount of times He is willing to be our advocate. While John wrote so that his spiritual children might not sin, he knew they would. Jesus knows this too and stands before God to advocate for us. As a man, He publicly affiliates Himself with sinners.

Is there a more powerful voice than that of Jesus Christ to go before the Father?

A New Hope: Our Beloved, Waiting for Us

Jesus, the God-man, our great high priest, right now is watching over us, ruling from heaven over all things. He is completely fulfilled and content as the second person of the Trinity, and yet He eagerly awaits eternity with His beloved. He is not in need of our presence, but He looks forward to it. The Psalms proclaim: 'Precious in the sight of the LORD is the death of his saints' (Ps. 116:15). What a

---

2   https://www.desiringgod.org/messages/jesus-christ-is-an-advocate-for-sinners

sweet union it must be for Jesus to be face to face with His beloved after having kept her and protected her through all the trials and temptations of this life. I imagine as a saint reaches the end of her appointed days, Jesus is eager to welcome her into His presence for all eternity. He must be excited to embrace her and show her how He advocated for her and arranged her life just as He did. How precious it must be for Him to show her His scars and the depths of His love for her. Things she once only believed by faith, at death she will behold by sight.

The end of the Scriptures provides for us a glimpse of the end of the age when all God's people are finally gathered to God Himself: 'And I saw the holy city, new Jerusalem, coming down out of heaven from God, prepared as a bride adorned for her husband. And I heard a loud voice from the throne saying, "Behold, the dwelling place of God is with man. He will dwell with them, and they will be his people, and God himself will be with them as their God. He will wipe away every tear from their eyes, and death shall be no more, neither shall there be mourning nor crying nor pain anymore, for the former things have passed away"' (Rev. 21:2-4).

At the end of all time God will dwell with His people again, just like in the garden of Eden. There will be no tears, for there will be no reason to cry. There will be no death, for it has been defeated. All the 'former things' will have passed away, and a whole new heaven and new earth will be established. Jesus Christ will be our bridegroom, and we will live with Him forever. There will be no temple in the city for God will dwell with His people. And the city will have no need of a sun or moon or any lights, because the glory of God will provide its light (see Rev. 21:22-27). Heaven awaits those whose names are written in the Lamb's Book of Life – forever in a perfect, pain-free, joy-filled existence where God's glory is not veiled, and we see Jesus face-to-face.

If you are a Christian, Jesus, your representative, king and advocate, is waiting for you now in heaven. This is the hope we have.

This forms a foundation of joy as we traverse, sometimes plodding, through this life, facing various trials and temptations. We have a Savior, who even right now, is seated at the right hand of God. Soon we will see Him not by faith, but by perfect sight.

QUESTIONS

MADE LIKE HIS BROTHERS

God intentionally raised up men in the Old Testament to foreshadow Jesus' life and His accomplishments. These men and their redemptive roles teach us about Jesus. He is our Last Adam, the One who would be the leader for a new group of redeemed people. He is our Eternal King, the fulfilment of the promise He made to be shepherd and king of His people forever. He is our great High Priest, the final and perfect sacrifice and mediator between man and God. And finally, He is our beloved, providing true hope and an eternity of love to His people.

1. How can the identity of Jesus give Jada (p. 113) hope?

2. Read Romans 5:18-19. Why was it so important for God to send a second man? Why did this second man have to be born of a virgin?

3. Adam was the original head of the human race. What people is Jesus the head of?

4. Read these passages that describe particular stories about David. How do we see Jesus pictured in them?

   a. 1 Samuel 17 (David and Goliath)

   b. 2 Samuel 9 (David and Mephibosheth)

5. Read the Great Commission at the end of Matthew 28. What is the first thing Jesus says to the disciples that has been given to Him? As a result of this ('therefore'), He then sends the disciples out. Why is it important that this direction given in verse 19 follows the fact stated in verse 18?

6. The role of the high priest was to be a mediator between God and man. The high priest was set apart for this unique role.

How does Jesus fulfil this role? Think about who He advocates on behalf of and to whom.

7. Read Revelation 21 about the re-created Garden of Eden. How does the hope of this new world with the risen Christ change the way you think about hope and disappointment?

8. In Revelation 21, we read about the bride who is prepared to meet her beloved. How does the image of the Lord Jesus anticipating meeting His bride spur you on to a greater faithfulness?

Chapter 6

The Word Became Flesh

A Christian colleague at work recently confided in you that she had an abortion several years ago when she was a college student. The guilt she carries now as a mom to two little girls has become a burden too heavy for her to carry. She has been fearful to tell anyone because she has so much shame. She believes that God must hate her, and on those days when she allows herself to think about what she did, she hates herself too. She believes that if God doesn't hate her, He must not care what happens in the world. In tears, she asks you which is true.

Hikers know the Aonach Eagach to be one of the UK's most dangerous treks. Hiking it, apparently, is even more difficult than pronouncing it. Just north of Glen Coe in the Scottish Highlands is this rocky ridge that has claimed the lives of many adventure seekers. To traverse this ridge, a hiker must scramble over rocks and rubble on a dangerous, narrow path for several kilometers. Much of the trail is barely wider than one's shoulders, but some of the ridge is even narrower than that. The most dangerous part of the trail is known as the Pinnacles, where the beaten path disappears into a thin series of jagged and pointed rocks that the hiker must climb and descend without falling off. The reward for reaching the top is 360 degrees of breathtaking beauty. But to enjoy it, the hiker has to stay balanced on the tip of this ridge. Steep cliffs on both sides of the trail promise the careless a certain demise. Only a sure foot keeps the traveler from a 3,000 foot rocky plummet on either side.

The missteps in expounding on the union of Jesus' divinity and humanity have led many unsuspecting men and women to a similar fate. Understanding this mystical union requires careful attention and sure footing. The traveler must beware that it's easy to fall off either side of the ridge. The potential for heretical disaster awaits, but the trip to the top, although it may seem slow, is worth it because the view is breathtakingly beautiful.

Narrow Path, Paved Slowly

The controversy about the nature of Jesus started when He was still on earth. Remember the crowds that surmised Jesus was an old prophet back from the dead? That confusion did not die when Jesus ascended into heaven. Early in church history, some began to teach the false idea that Jesus was just God in human form, and that God has manifested Himself in different ways at different times in history. This false idea, called modalism, argues that sometimes God appears as the Father, sometimes the Son, and sometimes the Holy Spirit. While this doctrine has been refuted based on the evidence of Scripture, there are still some denominations and televangelists who teach modified aspects of this heresy.[1]

---

1   There are a number of passages in Scripture that refute the claim that there is no Trinity, but instead God merely appears in different forms at different times. All references to the Father speaking either to or about the Son (Matt. 3:17, Matt. 17:5, Luke 3:22, Mark 9:7, Luke 9:35) or the Son praying to the Father (John 11:41-42, John 12:28, John 17, Luke 23:34, Matt. 27:46, Mark 15:34, Luke 23:46) are evidence against modalism.

In part to refute modalism, some set out to teach that God the Father and God the Son are distinct persons. Unfortunately, Arius, who we met in a previous chapter, stepped over the ledge of the cliff when he claimed that the Son being begotten by the Father meant that there was a time when the Father existed without the Son. He falsely concluded that the Son was a created being instead of the Creator of all things. This notion led him to conclude that Jesus was subordinate to the Father, instead of equal to Him. In 325 AD the Council of Nicaea denounced Arius' teaching and labeled it heretical. Truth prevailed in that battle over the church's understanding of the true nature of Christ; however, it was not the last conflict.

Soon after Nicaea, new controversy arose that the church was forced to address. In a push against Arianism, Apollinaris wanted to show Jesus was equal to the Father and fully divine. But he pushed too far and fell off the other side of the cliff when he began teaching that Jesus was fully God and only appeared human. Apollinaris said that Christ took on the shell of human flesh but His mind, will, and nature were divine, thus rejecting a comprehensive view of the humanity of Christ. The Council of Constantinople met in 381 AD, in part to consider the teachings of this theologian. They recognized he was not standing on solid ground but had descended into heresy.

Along came Nestorius, the Archbishop of Constantinople and an interesting figure in church history. He found himself in the middle of a controversy about how to refer to Mary, the mother of Jesus. She had been called *Theotokos*, a Greek word meaning 'God-bearer' in a nod to her role in the incarnation, but some argued that as an eternal being, God could not have been born. Nestorius suggested a new title for Mary (*Christotokos*, which means 'Christ-bearer'), but that title created even more controversy. It isn't clear whether Nestorius himself actually adhered to the doctrine later ascribed to him, or if he was just terrible at defending what he believed, but the doctrine of Nestorianism offered another theory to this lingering question of how to explain the exact nature of Christ. It essentially taught that the humanity and the divinity of Christ were independent of one another, such that the body of Jesus in effect held two different and distinct persons – one human and one divine. This teaching was also condemned. This time at the Council of Ephesus in AD 431.

The theologian Eutyches attempted to answer this mystery of the nature of Jesus, but he also veered off course, this time back to misunderstanding the humanity of Jesus. In response to the lingering debates in the church from Nestorianism, he argued that Jesus was not actually fully human. He said Jesus originally had two distinct natures – human and divine – but His humanity was usurped by His divinity, the greater one 'swallowing up' the finite one. We call this Monophysitism ('single nature'). His teaching caught on and the church fathers called a council again. This time they determined to settle the matter of the nature of Christ, and they met for one month in the late fall of 451 AD at the Council of Chalcedon.

Significant from this meeting was the rejection of many false doctrines about the nature of Jesus that had continued to linger in the church, leading many into dangerously unstable territory. One error was the belief that Christ had a single, divine nature and so was not fully human. The opposing camp, also in error, argued Christ was primarily human, and they lacked a right understanding of His divinity. The Council also refuted those who argued Jesus was a mixture of the two natures. Instead, they affirmed that Jesus is to be 'acknowledged in two natures, without confusion, without change, without division, without separation.'[2] This was such a significant and important meeting in church history that most church historians group periods of time as pre-Chalcedon and post-Chalcedon. Here is the statement they agreed upon, translated into English:

---

2   http://www.apuritansmind.com/creeds-and-confessions/the-chalcedonian-creed-circa-451-a-d/

Therefore, following the holy fathers, we all with one accord teach men to acknowledge one and the same Son, our Lord Jesus Christ, at once complete in Godhead and complete in manhood, truly God and truly man, consisting also of a reasonable soul and body; of one substance with the Father as regards his Godhead, and at the same time of one substance with us as regards his manhood; like us in all respects, apart from sin; as regards his Godhead, begotten of the Father before the ages, but yet as regards his manhood begotten, for us men and for our salvation, of Mary the Virgin, the God-bearer; one and the same Christ, Son, Lord, Only-begotten, recognized in two natures, *without confusion*, *without change*, *without division*, *without separation*; the distinction of natures being in no way annulled by the union, but rather the characteristics of each nature being preserved and coming together to form one person and subsistence, not as parted or separated into two persons, but one and the same Son and Only-begotten God the Word, Lord Jesus Christ; even as the prophets from earliest times spoke of him, and our Lord Jesus Christ himself taught us, and the creed of the fathers has handed down to us.[3]

This statement of truth is a helpful summary of the Biblical teaching on the nature of Christ, and the four 'without' statements are worth looking at more closely.

First, He is 'without confusion.' Confusion is what you get when your kids smash different colored Play-Doh together to create a muted third color. Jesus is not a third option, the result of mixing a divine and a human nature. He is also 'without change.' Jesus remains immutable, and the incarnation did not cause any substantial change in the divinity of the Son. In other words, at the incarnation the Son of God did not stop being what He always has been. He is 'without division,' which means neither of the two natures of Christ are divided or split. Jesus is not one-part God and

---

3   Ibid (italics mine).

one-part man (or any other division of either side). He is not like oil and water, with the oil rising to the top. And He is also 'without separation,' which refers to the fact that the divine nature and the human nature of Christ is a real union, not just one in which His divinity and His humanity agree to cooperate in a partnership. The union that happened when the divine and the human met in Christ is now an eternal union that will never be separated.

Jesus, Fully God and Fully Man

The theological term for the union of the divine nature and the human nature in the single person of Christ is the hypostatic union. Jesus Christ – uniquely – is one person with two natures. (Incidentally, hypostatic means *personal*, so it refers to the personal union of Jesus' two natures.) As we've seen, falling off either side of the cliff of this critical doctrine will cause you to land in dangerous, heretical territory. Standing confidently on the path of the truth taught in Scripture provides glorious views, and ones that we should pause to enjoy. We have already considered in individual chapters that Jesus was fully God and was also fully man, but the Bible teaches that Jesus was both at the same time and in the same physical body.

Judging from the amount of carnage found at the bottom of the two cliffs, we need to approach the Scriptures carefully, considering what they teach about the nature of Jesus. We'll start with Philippians 2, which lays the crucial foundation for our understanding of this mystical union.

Speaking of Jesus, Paul writes, '...though he was in the form of God, [he] did not count equality with God a thing to be grasped, but emptied himself by taking the form of a servant, being born in the likeness of men' (Phil. 2:6-7). Much has been misunderstood about Jesus by misinterpreting the Greek word *ekénōsen* that has been translated in this passage as 'emptied himself.' Some have argued that Jesus stopped being God when He came to earth as a man, referring to this passage to argue that Jesus 'emptied' Himself of His divinity. Many men have fallen into this heretical belief, called the kenotic theory. They argue at the incarnation Jesus set aside some of His divine attributes like omniscience, omnipotence, and omnipresence. They look to passages such as when Jesus said He does not know when He will return to earth for a second time as proof that He 'set aside' His omniscience or to the times He was tired to show He lacked omnipotence.

But Jesus did not empty Himself of any of His divine nature; rather He emptied Himself of His *rights* as God when He became a human being. Jesus did not *grasp on to* – take full advantage of – His equality with God, but rather voluntarily gave up His rights as God when He took on the likeness of men. He did not give up actually being divine. Instead He 'emptied himself *by taking the form of a servant*'. Paradoxically, when Paul wrote that Jesus 'emptied' Himself, this emptying was not a subtraction but an addition. Adding humanity to His divinity is considered an emptying.

An illustration may be helpful to understanding what this means, although all illustrations will be limited in their ability to explain this concept. The TV show *Undercover Boss* features a senior executive, often the CEO of a company, who takes on the identity of an entry-level employee in his or her own company. The undercover boss dresses like, acts like, and works alongside entry-level employees while a film crew tapes their interactions for the television audience. The drama escalates when the viewing audience knows what the unsuspecting employees do not know about the 'new' hire. The undercover CEO remains the boss of the company even though he looks like an average employee. In some episodes, the executive dresses like a blue-collar worker, stands at an assembly line, and punches a time clock. While he remains the CEO, he does not take advantage of – or 'grasp' – his rights as the boss. He does not utilize his personal secretary, his corner office, or his company car. He subjects himself to time-limited breaks and mundane tasks, but he is still CEO.

Similarly, but on a far grander scale and with infinitely more at stake, this is what Jesus did. He did not stop being God when He took on human form. He cloaked His divinity with humanity. To continue the metaphor, He put on His blue-collar clothes, but that did not mean He stopped being the boss. Somehow Jesus was still upholding the universe while He was lying in a manger. Christ added humanity to Himself. The *Undercover Boss* illustration is limited in its ability to fully convey the humility of Jesus taking on humanity. In addition, Jesus was not on an 'undercover' mission. For much of His ministry Jesus did not suppress the fact that He was God, but rather He made it clear and He wanted it to be understood that He was the prophesied Messiah, God's Son.

This is what the hypostatic union of Christ means. Jesus remained fully God in the incarnation, but He took on the form of a servant when He became a man. His deity was veiled, but He in no way ceased from being God. He embraced the limitations of humanity, like hunger pains, discouragement, and the need for rest. He embodied servanthood by doing things like washing the disciples' feet and being subject to ridicule. And eventually, He even obediently went to the cross. In other words, 'being found in human form, he humbled himself by becoming obedient to the point of death, even death on a cross' (Phil. 2:8). As God, Jesus could have called legions of angels to battle on His behalf at any moment. But as a servant found in human form, He perfectly fulfilled the mission He came to accomplish: salvation for man.

Eternally God, but Growth as a Man

In light of our consideration that Jesus was both fully God and fully man, we should carefully revisit what it means that Jesus grew as a human, both intellectually and developmentally, while still remaining fully God. He was no less divine when He was a newborn than He was as a teenager, but clearly Scripture shows a progression in His human intellect and emotions as He matured (Luke. 2:52). As a three-month-old Jesus did not possess the same knowledge that He had as a thirty-year-old. He had to begin life unaware of His surroundings. He had to learn to think and talk, just like He had to learn to crawl and walk. He had to grow into an awareness of who He was as His mind developed and He was able to self-conceptualize. His taking on humanity was not merely the second person of the Trinity being embodied with arms and legs. He subjected His mind to the limitations of humanity as well. It staggers our intellect to think that baby in the manger was God but was unaware that He was God. While it may seem strange for us to imagine Jesus as a child figuring out for the first time that He was quite unlike the other boys, for Christ to fully embrace His humanity, He had to subject Himself to normal human development.

Jesus had an increasing self-awareness of His divinity as He matured. In all likelihood, Mary would have explained to her son all the miraculous events surrounding His birth. We know He had a remarkable understanding of the Old Testament even as a boy, so He would have seen and understood that His life fulfilled all that was promised. Through this increasing self-awareness, He would have had a unique and intimate relationship with the Father, one unlike our own.

There is mystery to our understanding of what information Jesus had access to as a human and what He did not. Some instances in Scripture show He had supernatural knowledge (i.e. He knew the Samaritan woman had five husbands before He met her[4]), but He tells His disciples that only the Father knows when He will return to earth a second time (Mark 13:32). How do we rightly understand how the human embodiment of wisdom could have

---

4   John 4:18; see also Luke 2:47, John 1:47, John 11:14; Matthew 17:27; Luke 5:4-6; Mark 14:13.

lacked knowledge? We must remember the limitations of humanity that Jesus took on Himself. He subjected Himself to a mind that would grow and develop as He did not take advantage of all of His rights as God. He did not take advantage of all His rights of omniscience, but rather He limited His ability to know all things at all times while He was on earth, growing and developing like every other man.

In His divine nature, Jesus knew all things, but by self-imposing restrictions on His divine rights, He was able to fully embrace His humanity. Theologian Donald Macleod summed up this topic: 'Christ had to submit to knowing dependently and to knowing partially. He had to learn to obey without knowing all the facts and to believe without being in possession of full information. He had to forego the comfort which omniscience would sometimes have brought.'[5] In His humanity, Jesus had to trust His heavenly Father just as we do.

Jesus repeatedly spoke of doing only what the Father willed Him to do or say. He said, 'The Son can do nothing of his own accord, but only what he sees the Father doing. For whatever the Father does, that the Son does likewise' (John 5:19-20; see also John 7:16, John 12:49). Jesus knew what His Father's will was because His Father revealed it to Him. The sin that permeates not only our hearts but also our minds prevents us from hearing directly from the Father. Our sin separates us from God. This is a main reason that God gave us His written Word to communicate with us in an unfiltered, direct way. Jesus, however, was the Word who became flesh and was in perfect unity with the Father and the Spirit. He was not tainted with sin, and therefore direct and regular revelation from the Father was possible. The Father's direct revelation of supernatural knowledge preceded Jesus'

---

5   Macleod, *The Person of Christ*, p. 169.

words, thoughts, and actions. That direct revelation came to Jesus from the Father, as He was carried along by the Spirit.

Jesus was fully human. He grew and developed and perfectly obeyed the will of the Father. It had to be that way. Stephen Wellum writes, 'Without the eternal Son's fully human birth, growth, and development, we would not have an all-sufficient Savior whose sacrificial death achieved for us the full forgiveness of our sins and whose sympathetic service helps us to walk in the power of that forgiveness. The outer life of Christ presented to us according to the Bible's own terms demonstrates that he came into this world with a fully human nature to accomplish as a man all that God required of and planned for humanity.'[6] Jesus' sinless human life, developing from a baby to a boy to a man, fulfilled the necessary requirements both for our salvation and to provide the help His people need to follow Him.

TRANSCENDENT, IMMANENT GOD

To religions like Islam and some sects of Sikhism, the concept of God is of a being far away, distant, impersonal and removed considerably from human life and existence. Many people from these religions argue that God is so unlike us, we can never know what He is actually like. As mortal beings, we may never enter His presence or know Him in a personal way. Muslims argue we cannot have any assurance during this life that we will ultimately please God and be accepted into heaven. They believe man cannot know the mind of God, as He is so different from man.

Conversely, in some other religions God is often considered very near. In many cultures, people describe God as so near that He is in us and part of everything around us. Hindus believe there is something divine in everyone. In Western culture, those who think of themselves as spiritually-minded may also describe God's

---

6   Stephen J. Wellum, *God the Son Incarnate: The Doctrine of Christ* (Wheaton, IL: Crossway, 2016), p. 212.

presence as immanent. To liberal Christians such as the nineteenth-century theologian Friedrich Schleiermacher, the universe was merged into God and there existed no proper distinction between the created and the creator.[7] Schleiermacher influenced generations of liberal theologians, arguing beyond the omnipresence of God, and rather teaching that God was in and a part of all things. A contemporary of his from Scotland named W. Robertson Smith was once accused of denying the divinity of Jesus, and he responded with, 'How can they accuse me of that? I've never denied the divinity of any man, let alone Jesus.'[8]

The prophet Isaiah certainly would not have described the presence of the holy God as everywhere and in every man. He was given a vision of seraphim worshiping the holy God seated on His throne, and his response was one of fear. 'Woe is me!' he cried. 'I am ruined! For I am a man of unclean lips, and I live among a people of unclean lips, and my eyes have seen the King, the LORD Almighty' (Isa. 6:5, NIV). He did not have a casual attitude about approaching the holy God. Instead, he immediately recognized that his sin condemned him in the presence of God. Moses, who spoke directly with God, also understood this aspect of His character, especially after God told Moses no one could see His face and live (Exod. 33:20). Paul also described this transcendent aspect of God to Timothy when he wrote that God 'dwells in unapproachable light, whom no one has ever seen or can see' (1 Tim. 6:16). Far from the idea that God's presence casually resides among us, God's unmediated presence in Scripture elicits terror for the sinner. Nadab and Abihu, who disobeyed God's instructions for sacrifice at His altar and were immediately struck dead because of it (Lev. 10), certainly testify against a nonchalant approach to the presence of God.

---

7   Wilcox, Tice, and Kelsey, *Schleiermacher's Influences on American Thought and Religious Life*, volume 1 (Eugene, OR: Pickwick Publications, 2013) p. 264.

8   Miller Erickson, *Christian Theology* (Grand Rapids, MI: Baker, 2013), p. 675.

But in Jesus, we encounter divinity that remarkably is both transcendent and immanent. He is the holy and perfect God who has existed for all eternity, and yet He has come near to us, even becoming like us. The merging of Jesus' two natures into one person means we have one being who is infinitely complex and beautiful to whom we can direct our worship. Transcendent and immanent, He displays a beauty and magnificence that cannot be matched by any other god nor any other human being.

A god who is far off cannot satisfy the deep longings of our soul to know and be known by a personal God. Similarly, our souls were made to worship someone far more spectacular than even the best behaved, most benevolent human we know. Add to this splendor the love of God. God sent His Son to eternally take on human nature in a mysterious way because of a profound love for us. This is our God. He does not keep Himself far off and distant, unconcerned with His creation. But He is certainly never ordinary and common either. What a privilege to be able to know this God personally!

> Come behold the wondrous mystery
> In the dawning of the King
> He the theme of heaven's praises
> Robed in frail humanity
>
> In our longing, in our darkness
> Now the light of life has come
> Look to Christ, who condescended
> Took on flesh to ransom us[9]

Praise God that we can worship this transcendent, immanent God throughout eternity!

---

9   'Come Behold the Wondrous Mystery', Matt Papa, Matt Boswell, Michael Bleecker, 2013.

Eternally the God-man

A few pages back I gave an illustration to help us think about the incarnate God and likened it to a company CEO pretending to be a new employee. I cautioned that this illustration was limited in its ability to fully convey what it means that God became man. While it hopefully helped explain the concept that Jesus did not take advantage of His rights as God when He became man, it falls woefully short in helping us understand that when Jesus took on humanity over 2,000 years ago, He retains it even today. The CEOs on *Undercover Boss* went back to their jobs as company heads after recording the show. Jesus remains fully God and fully man for all eternity.

As you read this book, Jesus is reigning in heaven over all things (Matt.28:18, 1 Cor. 15:25, Eph. 1:22, Rev. 1:4-5) waiting for His appointed time to return to earth and gather all His saints for eternity. And He is doing so in His glorified, physical body. His human form was not a costume He put on, simply to be taken off when He returned to heaven. He did not wash it away or change back into His spiritual state after the taping was done. John wrote that the Word *became* flesh, not that He temporarily took on flesh. Paul even refers to Jesus in His current state when He wrote to Timothy, 'There is one God, and there is one mediator between God and men, *the man Christ Jesus*' (1 Tim. 2:5, emphasis mine).

As the God-man, Jesus will remain this way eternally. At His ascension as the disciples looked to the sky, the angels assured them that He would 'come back in the same way you have seen him go into heaven' (Acts. 1:11). He will one day return in His glorified body to gather His beloved bride.

We await His return and our eventual transformation into a body like His glorified one. 'Our citizenship is in heaven, and from it we await a Savior, the Lord Jesus Christ, who will transform our lowly body to be like his glorious body, by the power that enables him even to subject all things to himself' (Phil. 3:20, 21). All those who are in Christ will one day possess glorified bodies like that of Jesus. We do not know all that entails, although we can safely assume our new bodies will be free from the side-effects of sin, like disease and decay.

The Son of God has existed for all eternity and for the rest of eternity will also exist in a glorified body, having taken on the likeness of man. This is a God who has gone to extreme lengths to demonstrate His love for us. This is an all-powerful and holy God we can confidently worship for having come near to us for all eternity.

Our eternal Savior is not a far-away deity, detached from the world He created. He has come near to us, and He promises to remain near. As the eternal God-man, He is both our friend and our powerful advocate. He sympathizes with our weaknesses, and yet is strong and powerful enough to overcome them. There is no friend like the friend we have in Jesus.

What a Friend We Have in Jesus

As we grow in our understanding of this dual nature that only Jesus possesses, one obvious application is that our prayer life should soar. When we begin to grasp the depths of Jesus' empathy and love for us in that He will remain the God-man forever, we should feel no inhibition in asking God for all of our needs. In His nearness to us, Jesus relates to all our problems. When that freedom to ask of Him is coupled with His power to answer our prayers, the end result should be a dynamic prayer life. We should pray boldly. We should pray big prayers to a big God who has loved us in an infinitely big way. We should pray for His glory to cover the earth. We should pray for unreached people groups to experience revival and come to Jesus by the thousands. We should pray for God to work in us and through us in the spheres of influence we have.

Pastor Phil Ryken tells of a prayer meeting in Gilcomston South Church in Aberdeen, where he interned under Reverend William Still. Every Saturday night 60-70 people in this congregation gathered to pray 'all the way around Scotland, then through the British Isles, and then off to some other continent. Even after two hours of prayer, Mr. Still often closed the meeting lamenting that some continent or another had been left unprayed for.' Ryken wrote that it was typical for a church member to thank God for answering their prayers for things like the collapse of the Soviet Empire. Ryken writes, 'I was tempted to pull one of them aside and say, "You know, it was a little more complicated than that. The global economy had something to do with it, not to mention the arms race and the spiritual bankruptcy of communism. It took more than your prayers to pull down the Berlin Wall." I was tempted to say such things, but I knew better. Who is to say what part a praying church actually plays in world affairs?'[10] On the last day when all things are made clear to us, we will likely be astonished at how effective our prayers were; and seeing that we will be even more astonished at how little time we spent in prayer.

What a friend we have in Jesus,
All our sins and griefs to bear!
What a privilege to carry
Everything to God in prayer.
O what peace we often forfeit,
O what needless pain we bear,
All because we do not carry
Everything to God in prayer![11]

---

10   IX Marks journal. Phil Ryken. https://www.9marks.org/article/praying-as-a-church-for-the-world-and-your-city/. June 21, 2016.

11   'Friend in Jesus', Joseph M. Scriver, 1855.

QUESTIONS

THE WORD BECAME FLESH

Many theologians have mis-stepped in attempting to make sense of the dual nature of Jesus, but Scripture teaches that He is both fully God and fully man. The theological term for the personal dual nature of Jesus is the hypostatic union.

1. How can the truth that the Son of God became flesh give your colleague (p. 135) comfort?

2. Church history is full of men who led others astray into heretical beliefs about the nature of Jesus. The early church often had to meet to consider popular ideas and whether or not they were in line with Scripture. Pick one of these men to research on your own: Arius, Apollinaris, Nestorius, Eutyches. What did he teach that was incorrect about Jesus being fully God and fully man? How did the early church respond to his teaching? Are there any churches today who still teach remnants of his false theology?

3. The Council of Chalcedon recognized Jesus' dual nature as both fully God and fully man. They came up with a list of four descriptions: without confusion, without change, without division, and without separation. What do each of these phrases mean?

4. Philippians 2:6-7 helps us understand Jesus' dual natures as both fully God and fully man. This passage does *not* mean that Jesus emptied Himself of all that made Him God. How does the passage explain what it meant for Jesus to 'empty' Himself or as the ESV says 'make himself nothing'?

5. Does your explanation in question 3 fit with a Biblical understanding of Jesus being both fully God and fully man?

Does it make sense in light of Jesus as a child? As a young man? As an adult?

6. To some religions God is far away and unknowable to mere humans. To others, God is very near – in us and among us and in every part of creation. How does the hypostatic union of Christ fulfil our longings for God to be other than us (transcendent) and personally involved with us (immanent)?

7. Jesus is in heaven even now as fully God and fully man. What are some ways you can praise God for this fact?

Part 2

The Work of Christ

Chapter 7

Promises Fulfilled:
The Work of Christ

Recently you have been plagued with guilt and shame remembering past sins. You have a hard time believing God really could forgive you for some of the things you have done. You think about your past with regret constantly and continue to plead with God to forgive you. You hope eventually He will and that you won't carry these burdens forever. But you don't know how long until either of these things are a reality and you live with freedom.

U.S. Olympic pole vaulter Sam Kendricks recently claimed his sixth USA outdoor championship title in a row and set a new record for the highest pole vault jump by any American in history. As I was writing this chapter, he won his second World Championship in a row, a feat accomplished by only one other pole vaulter. Thousands of people who follow track and field admire Sam for both his outstanding accomplishments in the sport and his positive demeanor as a competitor. A video that went viral from the 2016 Olympics exemplified one reason why his fan base is so large and loyal. During his final practice warm up jump before the competition, the U.S. national anthem played in the Olympic stadium to honor the victory of an American teammate. Sam, an Army reserve officer, stopped his run, dropped his pole, and immediately stood at attention on the runway, forfeiting his final practice jump. From the White House the President publicly recognized his patriotism and performance, and thousands applauded him for honoring country over self. My friends know about Sam because he is my nephew, and they have patiently listened to me brag about him, have liked my embarrassingly-excessive social media posts about him, and have celebrated his success with me.

So far in this book we have carefully looked at the person of Jesus. Now we turn to consider what Jesus accomplished. If this book were written about my nephew, here we would begin to analyze the sport of pole vaulting and Sam's amazing feat of vaulting himself twenty feet into the air with only the support of a fiberglass pole. We would consider the goal (getting one's entire body over a horizontal bar) and the remarkable manner in which Sam accomplishes this task. The moment of victory happens in this sport when one crosses the highest bar without it falling off, but if we were discussing Sam's victories, I would not just tell you about the bar hight. I would tell you about the length of his pole, the position of his hands on it, and who his coach is (my brother in law!). While the person of Sam is tightly interwoven with his accomplishments, we could carefully zoom in on each separately.

This book is about something much greater than one man's physical feat. It is about what the God-man Jesus accomplished through His life, death, resurrection, and what He is doing even now as He reigns in heaven. He won something much more valuable than an Olympic medal. He won eternal reconciliation between the one, true, holy God and sinful men. Having looked at who Jesus is, this section of the book will describe what He has accomplished, how He did it, and what the ultimate purpose of it is.

The Paradox at the Center

At the center of the Christian faith is glorious paradox. The innocent suffered to ransom the guilty. Humiliation and shame led to exaltation and worship. Because of death, there is life. This seemingly inconsistent yet triumphant message is the crux of the Christian faith: because of the death of Jesus, we can have eternal life with God.

Since the beginning of time people have divided over this message, but of course religion does not have a monopoly on conflict. People divide over many things. You may remember some years ago 'drama divided a planet'[1] as the Internet lost its mind over the color of a simple dress. Seemingly the entire world took to social media to discuss 'the dress.' And yet even though millions of people saw the same picture, there was no collective consensus about whether the dress was blue and black or white and gold. Half of the world saw the dress one way, and the other half saw it another. The dress appeared different colors, depending on the person who saw it (and apparently their neurological associations). The dressmaker later confirmed the dress was, in fact, black and blue, despite the insistence of thousands that they saw a white and gold dress in the picture. For the record, even though I was adamantly in the white and gold camp, I managed to avoid the existential crisis that ensued for some millennials. (*What is color? What is truth? Does life even matter if we can't even tell the color of the dress?!*)

With much more sobriety than we approach a viral internet sensation, every person on the planet must decide what they see when they look at the cross. Scripture portrays the cross and the death of Jesus as the central theme of the Christian faith. This faith that proclaims victory and triumph does not laud military

---

1   Washington Post headline (February 27, 2015).

might or conquered nations, but instead boasts in the painful and shameful death of our main character. The Christian message is one of a *servant* King. His death produced results that may at first seem counterintuitive. We are no longer under the law because He obeyed every word of it. Our freedom came because of His arrest. He took on our guilt and exchanged it with His righteous perfection.

Scripture unashamedly teaches that while the world sees the cross as foolishness, it actually displayed God's infinite wisdom and power (1 Cor. 1:23-24). 'The cross is folly to those who are perishing, but to us who are being saved it is the power of God' (1 Cor. 1:18). The way you see the cross depends on more than your neurological associations; you can only see the power of the cross if you have been given the spiritual eyesight to see its truth. Through His life and His death on the cross, Christ earned salvation for His people who could never earn it on their own. We refer to this act of reconciling man with God as the atonement. The atonement is central to the cross and the Christian faith.

Restoration of Harmony

Recently, a Muslim friend started a conversation with a dear friend of mine and me about the gospel. Our Muslim friend told us how captivated he was by the teachings of Jesus. He said he wanted to follow Jesus and what He taught, but He disagreed with us about the cross and resurrection. While seeming to like Jesus, he firmly believed in Islam's teaching that Jesus was only a prophet and did not actually die on the cross. This man was content to disagree about the death of Jesus and said he preferred to focus simply on Jesus' life. My dear friend correctly responded that the crucifixion can't be separated from what Jesus taught. Jesus' teachings culminated in His death. Jesus Himself repeatedly taught His disciples that He, 'must go to Jerusalem and suffer many things from the elders and chief priests and scribes, and be killed, and on the third day be raised' (Matt. 16:21). Jesus didn't come to earth as a man only to teach. He came to die.

The center of Christianity is Christ. And the climax of the life of Christ is His death on the cross. We never want to neglect His teachings and His example, but we *must not* ignore His atoning death. The purpose of His life on earth as a man was to die as a substitute for His people. The original meaning of the word *atonement* referred to restoration of harmony between estranged parties. The atonement of Christ was a restoration of the relationship between God and His people. It made the way for sinners to be accepted by the holy God. Understanding the atoning work of Christ is fundamental to believing the good news offered to sinners. It is not a second-tier issue or one about which we can agree to disagree but still hold to the same gospel. The cross is at the core of the Christian message.

Of course, not all people agree to what is essential to the Christian faith. My Muslim friend did not agree that in order to accept Jesus' eternal life he must accept His atoning death. Liberal theologians likewise often disagree about the primacy of crucifixion for the Christian faith. Instead they also emphasize the teachings and example of Jesus. Perhaps they feel pressure to present to the world a Christianity that is less violent or embarrassing than one centered around a bloody cross. Or perhaps they don't want to tell their listeners they are sinners in need of a Savior. Instead of arguing about the color of the dress, they talk about the style and fit and the occasion for wearing it. Those are fine secondary issues when discussing the dress, but they don't answer the primary question of what color it is. Nor does a Christian faith that emphasizes the tolerance of Jesus or His wisdom or strong leadership capabilities answer the question of how sinful men and women can be made right with a holy God.

The harmony that exists between God and His people because of the death of Jesus is the basis for our eternal salvation. The death of Jesus is the reason we live without condemnation or fear.

It provides for our righteousness. It is the means by which we enter God's presence, and it is what broke our bondage to sin. It reconciles us with God and gives us eternal life. And rightly, we will praise Jesus for it for all eternity.

And they sang a new song, saying,

'Worthy are you to take the scroll
    and to open its seals,
for you were slain, and by your blood you ransomed people
for God
    from every tribe and language and people and nation,'
(Rev. 5:9).

Pictures to Remember the Promise

From the very beginning of time, God provided one path for reconciliation between Himself and man. In order for God to forgive sinners and for peace in the relationship, a blood sacrifice was necessary. 'Without the shedding of blood, there is no forgiveness' (Heb. 9:22). The cross of Jesus was the ultimate act of bloodshed for God's forgiveness of His people's sins. This should not come as a shock to us anymore than it would have to the first-century Jews. God had been foreshadowing pictures of a blood atonement ever since Adam and Eve realized their need for reconciliation with God. As God's people waited for the promised offspring to come defeat their enemy, they had centuries to offer sacrifices in obedience and faith, seeking forgiveness from God.

Children in God's Old Covenant community grew up with vivid images of the necessity of blood sacrifice for the forgiveness of sins. They would have regularly seen the best lambs being raised in order to be slaughtered. They would have known what the priests' hands looked like, when they were dripping in the blood of a sacrificed animal. They would have been familiar with the smell of the burnt offering and would have seen its smoke rising above the altar in faith that God's wrath would not linger on His people.

In the camp of Israel, one seeking God's forgiveness had to present an unblemished male lamb to a priest who would put his hand on the head of the dead animal and confess the transgression, transferring guilt from the Israelite to the innocent lamb. The priest then would slaughter the lamb and perform rituals to cover the altar with blood. He would sprinkle the lamb's blood on the sides of the altar, pool it at the base of the altar, and smear it at the top of the altar on the four 'horns.' The priest then cut up the lamb carcass and placed it on the burning wood on the altar. As the lamb was consumed as a burnt offering, it produced a 'pleasing aroma' to the Lord. The detailed instructions God provided for ceremonies and rituals – if done by faith – would cleanse the people of their sin and restore their harmonious relationship to God. Those who heard the cries of the lamb being sacrificed, touched its blood, smelled the smoke of the burnt offering, and saw the flames engulfing the carcass would certainly not have left thinking their sin was no big deal to God.

God gave multisensory, three-dimensional pictures of how He would ultimately deal with sin. These pictures foreshadowed how Eve's promised offspring would one day crush the head of the serpent. God commanded daily sacrifices for sins and also special holy days and ceremonies for this purpose. The Passover celebration, the Feast of Unleavened Bread, the Day of First Fruits and the Feast of Harvest were some of those days God used to teach His people about Himself and their sin. One special holy day foreshadowed God's judgment of sin and His rescue plan for sinners in a particularly dramatic way. The Day of Atonement was the most holy day of the year, and it was the day God's people saw most clearly the means by which God would ultimately address sin.

Day of Atonement

God gave His people a very important picture of this promised work, and He did so using two goats. One goat symbolized how God punishes sin, and the other goat represented God's removal of sin from His people. In theological terms, one demonstrates propitiation and the other expiation. These two theologically symbolic goats still describe God's full-frontal assault on the problem of sin. The Day of Atonement[2] looked forward to God finally opposing sin and banishing it forever.

PROPITIATION

At the root of God's punishment for sin we find His grieved heart. When God surveyed the vast wickedness of the Genesis 6 world, He 'regretted that he had made man on the earth, and it grieved him to his heart' (Gen. 6:6). Seeing His image bearers in rebellion against Him brought Him pain and regret. We learn from Genesis that God's wrath toward sin led Him to flood the entire world, causing the destruction and end of every living thing on the earth that was not safely and mercifully encapsulated inside Noah's ark. As the flood waters dried up, we might expect that God's anger did as well. Noah exited his ark with only a representative sampling of the life that had been on earth, and he entered the new creation to a fresh new start with God. But only *after* Noah built an altar to the Lord and offered on it some of every clean animal as a burnt offering did God say He would never again curse the ground because of man's sin. It was the offering that ultimately soothed God's wrath toward sin, not the flood waters (Gen. 8:21). Noah's first act in the new world after the flood was worship through sacrifice. This concept of regaining the favor of God by offering a pleasing sacrifice is what theologians call 'propitiation.' Propitiation is the appeasement of God's wrath, bringing us back into fellowship with

---

2   See Leviticus 16 for a full description of the Day of Atonement.

God. It brings about a change in God's disposition so that instead of looking at us as objects of wrath, He looks at us as objects of love.

In another example from the Old Testament, Job's friends also appeased God's wrath through a burnt offering. During Job's affliction, his foolish friends gave him heretical council that defamed the character of God. They needed forgiveness for speaking blasphemy about God. So God instructed the friends to sacrifice burnt offerings to the Lord and have Job pray for them (Job 42:7-9). God's anger toward them had to be turned away before Job's intercessory prayers for mercy were heard.

The sacrifices made by God's people throughout the Old Testament were meant to have an effect on God. They were intended to appease God's righteous anger toward sin. The sacrificial system of offering the blood of animals did not change anything in God's people, but rather it turned God's anger away from the sinner and enabled a restored relationship with Him (Lev. 4:35; 5:10, Heb. 9:22).

On the Day of Atonement, this concept was especially obvious to God's people. God designed this day for cleansing His people from their sins from an entire year. It was the most solemn of the holy days, and the only day of the year the high priest was able to enter the Most Holy Place, the physical location where God's invisible presence dwelled. In this holiest room of the tabernacle (and later the temple) was the Ark of the Covenant, a specially designed golden chest which held the 10 Commandments, Aaron's staff, and a pot of manna. On top of this sacred chest was the ἱλασμός (*hilasmos*) (Rom. 3:25, Heb. 9:5). This Greek word means 'propitiation,' but is often translated into English from the Septuagint[3] as the 'mercy seat,' or sometimes as the 'atonement cover.' A more exact translation may be 'place of propitiation.' Regardless of the translation, the concept is clear. In the presence

---

3   The Septuagint is the earliest Greek translation of the Hebrew Old Testament, dating back as early as the 3rd century BC.

of God when atonement for sins is made, we find mercy from God. This 'seat' was the golden top of the Ark, and on it were two cherubim facing each other and bowing toward the center. This 'throne of God' was the place where God communicated directly with Moses.

On this most holy day, God required a fast from both food and work, allowing no distractions among His people as they repented of their sins. This day was the only one of the year the high priest was allowed to enter the Most Holy Place, so he dressed only in a plain, white linen tunic, not his usual priestly robe which was covered in gold and jewels. On this unique day when the priest stood before the presence of God, he did so simply and humbly, as the saints are described in heaven (Rev. 7:9; 4:4).

The high priest would enter the Most Holy Place three times in all that day. The first time he entered carrying a censer full of hot coals from the altar and a dish full of incense. As soon as he entered the room, he was to scatter the incense on the coals, so that the inner sanctum was filled with sweet smelling smoke. This thick smoke created a veil that covered the high priest's eyes so he could not see the mercy seat. This smoke protected the high priest, because not even he could see the glory of God and live.

The second time he entered the Most Holy Place he carried the blood of the bull that had been sacrificed for himself and the other priests. He personally had to be forgiven of his own sins before he could represent the people, seeking God's forgiveness for their sins. He sprinkled the blood of the bull for the household of the priests on the mercy seat and in front of it. Only then was the high priest able to return to the altar and sacrifice the goat on behalf of the sins of the people. The third time the high priest entered the Most Holy Place he carried the blood of this theologically significant goat. He sprinkled the blood on and in front of the mercy seat on behalf of all the Israelites. After he left the Most Holy Place for the third time (not to return for another year), the high priest also sprinkled blood on the outer altar and the tabernacle, symbolically cleansing both the Israelite people and the house of God, so that God could continue to dwell with His people. The high priest's sprinkling of blood in faith before the presence of the Lord satisfied God's wrath toward His people's sin.

The Day of Atonement in all of its ritual and solemnity served as a picture of the sacrifices that would one day be offered by Jesus on our behalf. The author of Hebrews shows how Jesus is *our* perfect high priest who entered into the Most Holy Place (the actual presence of God, not just a tent) and entered by means of His own blood, not that of a bull. As His blood was sprinkled before the presence of God on our behalf when He died on the cross, propitiation was made *for us*. God's wrath is turned away from us eternally, and we find mercy. 'Through the greater and more perfect tent (not made with hands, that is, not of this creation) he entered once for all into the holy places, not by means of the blood of goats and calves but by means of his own blood, thus securing an eternal redemption' (Heb. 9:11-12).

John tells us Jesus' sacrifice was done out of God's great love for His people. 'In this is love, not that we have loved God but that he loved us and sent his Son to be the propitiation for our sins' (1 John 4:10). Jesus was the ultimate sacrifice, better than any bull or goat. His sacrifice was not merely symbolic. His death truly satisfied God's righteous anger toward sin and therefore opened the door for God's people to have fellowship with Him. His death was the final 'pleasing aroma,' eternally sufficient to turn God's wrath away from His people.

We must remember that God is the one offended by sin. He was the one dishonored by Adam and Eve's rejection of His good authority. He is the one we reject, blaspheme, and disobey, and He determines how sin's debt should be paid. Thankfully, out of His love, God took the initiative to pay the penalty for our sin. Propitiation changes God's posture toward sinful people. Jesus 'is the propitiation for our sins' (1 John 2:2). His sacrifice clears the way for us to be right with God.

EXPIATION

Propitiation serves as part of the concept of atonement, but, remember, there were two goats present at the Day of Atonement. A companion doctrine to propitiation is expiation, which refers to the removal of guilt by the payment or offering of an atoning sacrifice. At the Day of Atonement, after the blood of one goat was sprinkled on behalf of the people, the high priest would lay his hands on the head of the second goat, confessing the sins of the people. This 'scapegoat' was then led east, outside of the camp and far into the wilderness. As the goat left, the people's sins were symbolically removed, 'as the east is from the west' (Ps. 103:12). Outside the camp, the goat was doomed to die in the wilderness. The sins of God's people were punished, and their guilt was completely removed from them. Expiation involves taking away our sins in the same way the scapegoat was led into the wilderness bearing the iniquities of the people (Lev. 16:21-22).

The blood Jesus shed was foreshadowed by the first goat, as it turned the Father's wrath toward sin away. But Jesus was also our scapegoat. He took the sins of the people upon Himself. He bore them when He went outside the gate (Heb. 13:12) to die, forsaken by God. Because Christ removed the stain of sin from His people, they are forgiven. Because of the cross we are no longer defined by sin, nor do we have to be punished for our iniquity. Christ Himself has carried our sins away.

As God removed the guilt of sin from us, the problem of sin was completely and comprehensively addressed and put away forever. God closed the chapter on His people's sin, and He will never open it again. He gave us several images to help us understand this concept: He washes the scarlet stain of sin into something white as snow (Isa. 1:18, 1 John 1:9), casts all our sins behind His back (Isa.

38:17), and blots them out and forgets them (Isa. 43:25, Isa. 44:22, Jer. 31:34, Heb. 8:12, Heb. 10:17). In God's eyes, He no longer sees our sin as He hurls them into the depths of the sea (Micah 7:19). Those who are in Christ no longer even bear the mark of sins that once were. I can think of no better news to encourage my soul than this fact: because of the cross of Jesus, our sins have been forgiven and forgotten. Because of the cross, the power of sin is broken. The image of God in us is restored and we can live lives of freedom that bring God glory.

If you are in Christ but struggle to believe God has forgiven you for all your sins, meditate on this truth that Jesus has absorbed every drop of God's anger toward your sin, and He has carried it far away from you. No matter how shameful or unforgivable you think your sin may be, God's mercy to you in Jesus is greater. God has no lingering frustration or irritation with you. He is not embarrassed of you. He does not have the A+ pupils He is proud of and the failing students He hides away somewhere. If you are in Christ, you are loved and accepted fully by God, despite your sin. If the guilt you carry prevents you from intimacy with God, let the atonement of Christ wash over you afresh. Your sins have been paid in full, and there is no condemnation now for those who have been washed by the blood of the lamb.

> My sin, oh the bliss of this glorious thought My sin, not in part, but the whole,
> Is nailed to the cross, and I bear it no more, Praise the Lord, praise the Lord, O my soul![4]

VICTORY DISPLAYED

Sin was defeated when Jesus died on the cross. After His death, He was taken off the cross and was buried. A stone was rolled in front of His grave to prevent anyone from entering His tomb, and soldiers

---

4   'It is well with my soul', Horatio Spafford, 1873.

guarded it to stop His zealous followers from any attempt to steal the body (Matt 26:62-66). But Jesus' story was far from over. In a beautiful display of Jesus' high esteem of women, He commissioned Mary Magdalene, healed by Jesus of demon possession and steadfastly devoted to her Lord, to be the first to herald the greatest message mankind was ever to hear: Jesus of Nazareth had gone into the grave dead and come out alive (John 20:17-18).

If sin was defeated at the cross, what was the purpose of Christ's resurrection from the dead? Was it merely a helpful way to wrap up the Gospels? Or was it *necessary* to accomplish our salvation? According to Paul, it was vital. In his first letter to the Corinthians, Paul made clear to those who doubted the physical bodily resurrection of Jesus, 'If Christ had not been raised, your faith is futile, and you are still in your sins' (1 Cor. 15:17).

Why would our faith be futile if Christ had not been raised from the dead? In this passage of 1 Corinthians, Paul directly links our eventual resurrection with Christ's resurrection from the grave. Here Jesus is called the 'firstfruits of those who have fallen asleep' (1 Cor. 15:20). He was the first among many. If not for His resurrection, those who would follow (all of those in Christ) would also remain dead in the grave. If Christ had remained in the grave, the last Adam would have been no more hope to us than the first.

Much like how the Day of Atonement pictures the way God will deal with sin, Paul here is referencing the symbolism of another festival commanded by God that the Jewish people would have celebrated for centuries. 'Firstfruit' may not be a term we use regularly, but it would have been a very familiar part of Jewish vernacular in Paul's day. Every year the Jewish people celebrated the Feast of First Fruits in the Spring, around the time the barley harvest was ripe. This feast was a celebration of the first fruit of the crop, a representation of the whole crop that was to be harvested that season. This ritual was the first of three harvest festivals commanded by God to thank Him for their provisions, and as all of the Old Testament does, it also foreshadowed the work of the Messiah.

According to Levitical law, the priest would sacrifice a Passover lamb on the 14th of Nisan. On the next day, the Festival of Unleavened Bread began, in remembrance of how quickly the enslaved Israelites left Egypt – without even time to put yeast in their bread. And on the third day, they began the First Fruit celebrations. According to the law God gave governing the celebration, when the first of the harvest was reaped, the people were to "bring the sheaf of the firstfruits of your harvest to the priest, and he shall wave the sheaf before the LORD, so that you may be accepted (Lev. 23:10). A sheaf is a bundle of plants bound together after reaping. A presentation of the firstfruits before the LORD was a symbol to the people of their acceptance by God.

God's people performed this ceremony each year for centuries in obedience to His command and as a picture of how they would ultimately find acceptance by God. The crucifixion of Christ occurred on the 14th of Nisan – the same day the Passover lamb was sacrificed. The 16th of Nisan – the third day – was the Festival of First Fruit, the same day Jesus rose from the dead. Don't miss this picture. The priests and the people were in the middle of the festival God had given them (along with a promise that as they did it, they would find acceptance before God). And then sometime around 30 AD, right in the middle of the ritual was Jesus – actually doing the work that was being symbolized. He is the first of those raised from the dead, and it is because of His work that we are accepted before the Lord. Those in Christ are among the harvest that will one day be gathered before God, our first fruit (Jesus) being waved before the Father to show our acceptance.

Christ's resurrection displayed to the universe that God's rescue plan worked, and justification of sinners was now possible because salvation had been fully accomplished. This is why Paul writes that Jesus 'was raised for our justification' (Rom. 4:25). God's wrath for His people's sin fully terminated when Jesus declared, 'It is finished' moments before His death on the cross (John 19:30). At the resurrection, all could see Jesus' death was an acceptable and sufficient sacrifice.

John Piper explains how the resurrection displayed the victory of Jesus. He said, 'When Christ died and shed his blood for our transgressions, he atoned for the sins that killed him. Since those sins are now covered and paid for, there is no reason for Christ to remain dead. His death was solely to pay for our sins. When they were perfectly paid for, there remained no warrant for his death anymore. It would be unjust to keep him in the grave.'[5]

In raising Jesus from the dead, God showcased His magnificent power – even over death, the inevitable penalty for sin. 'We know that Christ, being raised from the dead, will never die again; death no longer has dominion over him' (Rom. 6:9). It also showed God's triumphant defeat over Satan and evil. Satan's dominion over the earth was broken at the cross, and God showed Himself eternally victorious when Jesus overcame Satan's greatest weapon – death – and rose from His grave.

THE KINGLY CORONATION

Jesus was on earth forty days after the resurrection. He appeared to many in His glorified body, complete with scars from His death on the cross. He taught and ate, and He appeared in and disappeared from rooms at will. He could have disappeared from earth and returned to heaven in the same manner, without much fanfare. But instead He gathered the disciples together for one last mountaintop worship service. He then ascended in a dramatic fashion with the disciples watching and angels narrating.

---

5   Sermon at Bethlehem Baptist Church on Romans 4:22-25, October 3, 1999. https://www.desiringgod.org/messages/why-was-jesus-put-to-death-and-raised-again

The Nicene Creed says of Christ, 'He ascended into heaven and sits at the right hand of God, the Father almighty, from where he will return to judge the living and the dead.' Our churches proclaim this truth, but do we understand the significance of the ascension? I'm afraid for many, it is more of an afterthought that is present but tangential to the 'real' work of salvation. It is almost as if the ascension were a helpful asterisk akin to a 'where are they now' blurb about a former celebrity.

The pomp and circumstance surrounding Jesus' departure from earth was His invitation to the disciples to watch His heavenly coronation as king. The Son of God incarnate left heaven to become a dependent baby, born from Mary's womb. And at Jesus' ascension, He returned to heaven with a qualitatively different status than when He left – as the God-man, the newly crowned King of the universe. Because of what He accomplished in His earthly life, He had won the right to rule over all things. As He ascended, He instructed His disciples, 'All authority in heaven and on earth has been given to me. Go therefore and make disciples of all nations, baptizing them in the name of the Father and of the Son and of the Holy Spirit, teaching them to observe all that I have commanded you' (Matt. 28:18-20).

He wanted the apostles on whom the church would be founded to see Him ascend to heaven as the God-man who would reign eternally as King. This gave them authority and confidence to face the intense persecution and trials they were all unknowingly about to face. They left that mountaintop experience and returned to Jerusalem 'with great joy.' They assuredly knew where the One who they served had gone: to sit ruling on His heavenly throne.

The disciples needed to be assured that now that Jesus was in heaven, He could fulfil the last thing He said to them: 'And behold, I am with you always, to the end of the age' (Matt. 28:20). When Jesus was on earth, He could only occupy one physical moment and space in time. Now that He was in heaven, He could – by His

Spirit – be with all His disciples at the same time, even though they were in different places and doing different things. The Spirit who would soon be sent to be with the disciples would provide direct help to each of the apostles. Jesus promised them He would 'teach you all things and bring to your remembrance all that I have said to you' (John 14:26). Imagine the comfort the disciples felt knowing the Spirit would be with them wherever they went. Our God is one who is personal and loving, and He promises to be with us at all times and through all situations. This knowledge must have given the apostles great comfort and hope in the midst of affliction, just as it should give hope to you and me.

Jesus also promised the Spirit would come in power and would *em*power the disciples. 'But you will receive power when the Holy Spirit has come upon you, and you will be my witnesses in Jerusalem and in all Judea and Samaria' (Acts 1:8). Of course the Spirit did come (on the Festival of Weeks or Pentecost, another significant day from the Levitical law), and He did empower the apostles to preach the Good News, perform miracles, and persevere to the end of their lives, even despite significant opposition and persecution. When Jesus asked the Father to send the Spirit, He knew He was giving the disciples a powerful gift of His own presence.

At His ascension, Christ took on the work of King, one who would rule and reign over all His creation. He accomplished the work of earning salvation for His people, but He did not stop working on their behalf.

A Work That Continues

Jesus is in heaven now, interceding for us, advocating on our behalf, watching and ruling over our lives, and praying for our safe arrival home to Him one day in heaven.

He said of His departure from earth, '...from now on the Son of Man shall be *seated* at the right hand of the power of God' (Luke 22:69). This sitting at the right hand of God refers to the position of honor and power the LORD reserved for the Messiah in Psalm 110. 'The LORD says to my Lord: Sit at my right hand, until I make your enemies your footstool' (Ps. 110:1). In referencing this Psalm, Jesus had taught that His work on earth was almost finished and He was going to rule as rightful King of the universe.

But a short while after the ascension, as Stephen was preaching the Good News of Jesus, he was cast out of Jerusalem and stoned by those who opposed the message. As Stephen's own martyrdom approached, he gazed into heaven and saw Jesus *standing* at the right hand of God (Acts 7:55-56). So which is it? Jesus was not sitting down next to His father. He was standing – the position of prayer – interceding for His beloved brother Stephen. While Jesus occupies the seat of honor as the King of the universe, He is actively working for us even now, just as He was for Stephen.

Christ's present heavenly intercession may be the most under-appreciated aspect of Jesus' work by us, and that is to our detriment. Our Savior lives to intercede for us. We should be praying with confidence and living boldly in light of the truth that Jesus has accomplished all we need for salvation and is now actively working to keep us and protect us until He can bring us safely home.

QUESTIONS

PROMISES FULFILLED

The center of Christianity is of course Christ. And the climax of the life of Christ was His death on the cross. The work of Christ in securing salvation for His people is called the Atonement. The Old Testament rituals prescribed on the Day of Atonement previewed how God would treat sin through propitiation and expiation. Jesus is our propitiation. In Christ, our sin was expiated at the cross. His work also includes His resurrection from the dead, His ascension into heaven, and His present heavenly intercession on our behalf.

1. How can understanding the atonement reorient your thinking and help you accept God's full forgiveness for all of your sin (p.175)?

2. Why is a faith that downplays Jesus' death on the cross insufficient for our salvation?

3. What are the theological terms associated with the two goats at the Day of Atonement?

4. Write in your own words what happened to each of those goats. What was being foreshadowed in each?

5. Read Leviticus 16. Why did the high priest have to offer a bull on the Day of Atonement?

6. Read Hebrews 9. How is Jesus like the high priest? How is He a better high priest? Why was it necessary for 'the copies of heavenly things to be purified with sacrifices' (v. 23)?

7. Why do we no longer offer blood sacrifices of bulls and goats?

8. What does Jesus' resurrection show? Why was it necessary?

9. What does 'firstfruits' mean in 1 Corinthians 15:20? What is the other fruit if He is the first? How does the former represent the latter?

10. Why is it better – even necessary – that Jesus ascended into heaven? How do we benefit from Jesus' position on His throne?

11. If you are a Christian, how does knowing that Jesus atoned for your sins give you confidence when you approach God in prayer? How does it help you when you are struggling with sin?

Chapter 8

Punishment in Our Place:
Penal Substitution

Sharon recently received a shocking health diagnosis. She has stage 3 breast cancer, and the doctors want to start treatment immediately. Her relatively peaceful and easy life has been suddenly turned upside down, and she says that she feels the foundations of her faith starting to crumble. Previously she had looked at her material blessings and health as God's blessings in her life and proof that He loves her. Now she is starting to wonder if God is punishing her for something. Is she right?

How would you describe the main theme of the story *Beauty and the Beast*? Is it that appearances can be deceiving? Gaston, the handsome prince, loves only himself, while the hideous beast actually turns out to be the hero. The teapot and silverware are certainly not what they first appear to be. Or is the theme one of sacrifice? Belle sacrifices her life for her father's, while the Beast has to learn to let go of his only potential for love when he releases Belle from capture. Or is the central theme one of finding community? Belle does not fit in with the townspeople, but ironically, she finds a home in the dilapidated castle, where the unusual occupants offer her friendship and acceptance. All of those storylines are present in the narrative, and part of the appeal of *Beauty and the Beast* lies in how each of these themes weaves into the story and finds resolution in the single act of the Beast's victory over Gaston. But in the final scene when the Beast dies defending Belle, we know for sure at the heart of *Beauty and the Beast*, it is a love story. It is a tale as old as time, they say. The beautiful and intelligent Belle and the ugly and harsh Beast fall in love, but just as we realize this love has begun to blossom, the Beast is killed by Gaston. The story appears to have a very tragic ending. It seems that the bad guy has won and true love has died. Only, it is love that actually breaks the curse that has kept the Beast and his entire castle imprisoned. Belle and the Beast's love brings the Beast back to life and turns the dilapidated castle into a beautiful home.

Since the first century, Christians have understood Jesus accomplished something significant through His crucifixion, but they have debated exactly what it was and how it happened. The cross of Christ achieved many things, but there is one theme that we find consistent throughout Scriptures. In other words, there are several storylines but one main theme—one idea that gets to the heart of what Jesus actually accomplished at the cross.

It would be good for us to remember from the outset that Scripture is clear about the cross and its accomplishments, and there have been followers of Jesus since His ascension that have clearly understood what He did on our behalf. But popular opinion on any topic is not always right, and the work of Jesus is no different. The Holy Spirit patiently directed the church through the ages to gain an increased understanding of not only who Jesus is but also of exactly what He accomplished. Remember that even though Scripture is clear, the church wrestled for over one hundred years and through multiple councils on various heresies before finally clarifying the Biblical teaching that Jesus had dual natures as both God and man.

The Journey to the Center

As early as the first century, Clement of Rome wrote beautifully of Jesus' work on our behalf: 'because of the love he had towards us, our Lord Jesus Christ gave his blood for us in accord with the will of God: his flesh for the sake of our flesh, his life for our lives.' Clement and many early Christians (including the writers of the Old Testament) understood that at the cross Jesus was a blood sacrifice on our behalf.

But not all were as theologically accurate as Clement. For several centuries, the **ransom theory** of Christ's atonement was widely used to explain Christ's work. The idea was championed by Origen in the third century and the Cappadocian Fathers in the fourth century. They argued the human race was in bondage to the *devil* because of sin, and God redeemed mankind by paying a 'ransom' to the devil. Similar to a kidnapper who demands payment in exchange for freedom, this theory argues Jesus' death was payment to Satan to win back God's people who were under Satan's dominion because of their sin. Some of the most misguided theologians argued that God tricked the devil into accepting this payment, and once it was accepted, God raised Jesus from the dead. The ransom theory rightly portrays Jesus' death as payment on behalf of His people, but it misses to whom that payment was made. And in response to those who argue God tricked Satan, God's character is one of unblemished truth. Tricking, conniving, or deceiving anyone – even His adversary – is in opposition to His character.

One of the most popular modern views spun from the ransom theory is called **Christus Victor**, put forth first by Lutheran theologian Gustav Aulén in 1931. This view argues that Christ 'fights against and triumphs over the evil powers of the world, the 'tyrants' under which mankind is in bondage and suffering.'[1] Theologians who argue for this theory claim Christ's death was primarily important because it defeated the powers of evil in this world. This evil had kept the world in the dominion of darkness since the fall, and 'the work of Christ is first and foremost a victory over the powers which hold mankind in bondage: sin, death, and the devil.'[2] God's glory certainly was displayed at the cross in His defeat of evil, but this theory does not comprehensively address all that was accomplished at the cross. It highlights the cosmic war between good and evil, but it does not address personal sin, separation from God, or the impossibility of man atoning for his own sin. It frames man's greatest problem in terms of good and evil in the universe, not sin and rebellion in our own hearts.

The ransom theory was seriously confronted as insufficient to fully explain the atoning work of Christ in the 11th century when Anselm of Canterbury wrote *Cur Deus Homo* ('Why God Became Man'), which challenged the church's thinking on Christ and ignited a fundamental change in its theological direction. Anselm rejected the idea that God owed something to the devil and instead argued that because of sin, the debt was actually owed by man *to God*. This idea is called the **satisfaction theory**. Anselm rightly framed man's problem as a debt to God that cannot possibly be repaid by sinful man. John Stott summarized Anselm's work on the necessity of the incarnation like this: 'No one ought to make satisfaction except man (who has defaulted) and no one can except God.'[3]

Anselm missed the center mark of the atonement, though, when he articulated his understanding of God's remedy for the problem of sin. Anselm reasoned our sin was an affront to God's

1   Gustav Aulén, *Christus Victor: An Historical Study of the Three Main Types of the Idea of Atonement* (New York City, NY: Macmillan, 1958), p. 4.

2   Ibid p. 20.

3   John R. W. Stott, *The Cross of Christ* (London: IVP, 1986), p. 90.

honor. Because of our disobedience, we have all defrauded God of the glory He deserves. Anselm argued Jesus restored God's honor through His sinless, perfectly obedient life, and He did so as a substitute for us. For those who do not accept Jesus' obedience on their behalf, God enacts eternal punishment. 'It is necessary either that the honor taken away be repaid, or else that punishment follow.'[4] Anselm understood correctly that Jesus served as a substitute for us and that His perfect obedience was a necessary aspect of the atonement. But Anselm neglected something significant. Scripture teaches that God's remedy to the problem of sin is not only perfect obedience, but God's righteousness demands *punishment* for our sins. Anselm's theory neglects to define Jesus' death as a satisfaction of God's wrath. While the difference may seem slight between believing that Jesus accomplished salvation through obedience or through punishment, the theological implications are significant and speak directly to the heart of what happened at the cross. Did Jesus die as a mere victim at the hands of the Jewish authorities or was His love so great that He was willing to take the punishment for all of our sin? And was that punishment from men or was the wrath of a holy God poured out on His Son? More simply put, is the problem of sin answered only by Jesus' obedience, or also by His punishment? To Anselm, it was only God's honor that was restored by substitutionary obedience, and also not His justice by a substitutionary penalty.

Another prominent theory throughout church history is the **moral exemplar** view of Christ's work. This theory, born out of Thomas à Kempis and his 15th century book *The Imitation of Christ*, showcases Jesus as the supreme model of godly living. This book was extremely popular during its time. In it, Kempis argues for people to seek personal holiness, born out of a love for Christ and a desire to follow His moral standard for living. He writes, 'the noble

---

4   St Anselm, *Cur Deus Homo* (Fort Worth, TX: RDMc Publishing, 1903), Book 1, Ch 13.

love of Jesus inspireth us to do great things, and ever impelleth us to long for perfection.'[5] Kempis's influence on modern theologians can be seen most clearly in those whose view of salvation focuses on the inner character of man being capable of being 'good' apart from conversion. These people may believe a divine spark or light exists in each of us, given by God for the purpose of loving and serving each other. They believe man is basically good and has the ability in Himself to imitate Christ. Those who subscribe to this view are often inspired by Jesus' life, but downplay the necessity of His dying in the place of sinners. His death was noble, but not a payment to God. People should strive to be more like Jesus, they argue, because He was a great example to us all. Therefore, Jesus should serve as a catalyst in society for good, as men and women seek to live lives of love as they follow Him.

Remnants of this view can still be seen among those who preach a social gospel that emphasizes doing good to others and neglects the Bible's teaching that the wages of sin is death. Mr. Rogers, famous for his TV series *Mr Rogers' Neighborhood*, taught that God is the great appreciator of us all and His love overcomes evil. As a universalist, he did not believe in the salvation of sinners, but rather taught that all men and women are capable of good if we stoke the divine spark in us. While the moral exemplar view draws inspiration from the life of Jesus in an often-compelling way, à Kempis and others like him neglect to deal seriously with the sin nature in all of our hearts and the vast separation between God and man that results from it.

There are aspects to each of these views that are Biblical and true. For example, the Bible teaches that Jesus did pay a debt to God we could not pay on our own (satisfaction theory). Scripture teaches that Jesus triumphed over evil powers, and put them to shame (Col. 2:15), destroying the power of death (Heb. 2:14) and the works of the devil (1 John 3:8) (Christus Victor). He is without question our greatest example in life, and the one we

---

5   Thomas à Kempis, *The Imitation of Christ* (London: Collins, 1957) p. 5.

should attempt to emulate, especially when we are treated unjustly (1 Pet. 2:21-24, Eph. 5:1-2) (moral exemplar view). But there is an explanation that more accurately gets to the heart of the gospel... one that hits the center of the bullseye... one that most clearly and comprehensively explains what happened on the cross.

The Center of the Cross

The most comprehensive and Biblical view of Christ's atoning work is called penal substitution. Sometimes called vicarious atonement, it is the idea that Jesus was punished in the place of sinners, satisfying the demands of justice and God's wrath so that God can forgive sin. One author defined it this way: 'The doctrine of penal substitution states that God gave himself in the person of his Son to suffer instead of us the death, punishment and curse due to fallen humanity as the penalty for sin.'[6]

Penal substitution can be summarized in two distinct and necessary parts: He was *punished* (penal) for sin, and He was a *substitute* for the sinner. At the cross, God 'made him who had no sin to be sin for us' (2 Cor. 5:21). As Jesus took on our sin and bore it on our behalf, both God's perfect justice and His wrath toward sin were satisfied. Remember His perfect justice would not allow God's forgiveness of sins unless a just penalty for sin was enacted. He could not ignore sin and remain a just and holy God. The cross was that just punishment. Because of it, God could forgive. In addition to this holy requirement for justice, God had a holy wrath toward sin. Man's sin had been kindling God's righteous anger since the fall, and while the blood sacrifices of the Old Testament appeased God, they did not satisfy His virtuous indignation for our rebellion. They merely served as placeholders until the cup of God's wrath (Jer. 25:15-29) could be fully poured out on Jesus, our

---

6   Jeffery, Ovey & Sach, *Pierced for Our Transgressions: Rediscovering the Glory of Penal Substitution* (Wheaton, IL: Crossway, 2007).

perfect substitute and the only one who was able to bear the totality of God's wrath.

The Protestant Reformation in sixteenth-century Europe helped 'rediscover' this doctrine and led the church to broadly understand and embrace the idea that Jesus' death on the cross included both punishment and substitution. Martin Luther, who was influenced by Anselm and his satisfaction theory, saw the scriptural merit for combining the concept of Jesus' satisfaction with the understanding that He was also punished in our place for our sin. Luther said, '...if God's wrath is to be taken away from me and I am to obtain grace and forgiveness, someone must merit this; for God cannot be a friend of sin nor gracious to it, nor can he remit the punishment and wrath, unless payment and satisfaction be made.'[7] He went on to argue that no one is capable of fully repaying the penalty for sin 'except that eternal person, the Son of God himself, and he could do it only by taking our place, assuming our sins, and answering for them as though he himself were guilty of them.'[8]

John Calvin aided the church's understanding of this critical doctrine, perhaps more than any one individual outside of the inspired authors of Scripture. Among many helpful things, he wrote, 'For we could not believe with assurance that Christ is our redemption, ransom, and propitiation unless he had been a sacrificial victim. Blood is accordingly mentioned wherever Scripture discusses the mode of redemption. Yet Christ's shed blood served, not only as a satisfaction, but also as a laver to wash away our corruption.'[9]

As the storyline of Scripture unfolds through its various historical accounts and genres from Genesis to Revelation, we see the main theme of punishment and substitution from beginning to end. It was imaged and foreshadowed in the Old Testament and

---

7   Sermons of Martin Luther, vol. 2, p. 344.

8   Ibid.

9   John Calvin, *Institutes of the Christian Religion*, II.xvi.6.

brought to full light and explained in the New Testament. It is the foundation on which we are able to confidently stand before God.

> It was my sin that held him there
> Until it was accomplished
> His dying breath has brought me life
> I know that it is finished
>
> Why should I gain from his reward?
> I cannot give an answer
> But this I know with all my heart
> His wounds have paid my ransom.[10]

Regrettably, the doctrine of Penal Substitution has fallen on hard times again. There are some vocal liberal theologians even inside the Protestant tradition who have argued that God did not need a blood sacrifice to forgive men for their sins. They argue penal substitution makes God out to be no better than the ancient pagan gods who demanded child sacrifices. *Isn't the greatest commandment to love? How is the death of an innocent man an act of love? Doesn't the all-powerful, all-knowing God have the ability to just forgive, without a blood sacrifice?* They have even labeled the idea that Jesus, God's Son, was punished in our place as 'cosmic child abuse.'

Are they right to argue that penal substitution is contrary to the character of God? Or that the doctrine makes God out to be some kind of blood-thirsty tyrant? To answer these questions, we must consider whether penal substitution is one of many minor storylines in Scripture or the main theme of it. Let's look at the theme of penal substitution and how it runs throughout the entire Bible story.

---

10   'How Deep the Father's Love for Us', Stewart Townsend, 1990.

Smitten by God

As mentioned previously, after the first sin, an animal is killed to cover the nakedness of Adam and Eve. Their sin caused the world's first bloodshed, and it gave us an early sketch of the concept of atonement – a covering for our nakedness and shame. As early as Genesis 4, we see animal sacrifices being made to God. Abel brought to God the firstborn of his flock while Cain brought an offering of fruit of the ground. Abel's sacrifice was done in faith, while Cain's was not, and so the former was accepted by God, but he had no regard for the latter. While we are not given details at this point in the story, we do see blood sacrifices being made that are accepted by God.

A few chapters later as soon as Noah emerged from the ark into a new world, he offered an animal sacrifice. These animals, who would certainly have been on the endangered species list, were slaughtered and sacrificed to God. Remember God had given Noah specific commandments regarding the number of animals on the ark. We must reason then that they were put there so that Noah would have a sacrifice to make to God when the flood waters subsided. Even though God had punished the creation with catastrophic destruction, a blood sacrifice was still necessary for sinners to enter this new creation. The sacrifice was 'pleasing' to God, and He promised to never again destroy the earth in that manner.

Later in Genesis, the images get clearer. God promised Abraham he would father many nations, but his wife Sarah experienced decades of lonely barrenness. She was nearly 90 years old when she finally gave birth to the promised son Isaac. God tested Abraham's faith by telling him to sacrifice the child, but as soon as Abraham proved his trust in God, God saved Isaac and provided a substitute sacrifice of a ram. Genesis 22 records this: 'And Abraham went and took the ram and offered it up as a burnt offering *instead of his son*. So Abraham called the name of that place, "The Lord will provide"; as it is said to this day, "On the mount of the Lord it shall be provided'" (Gen. 22:13-14, emphasis mine). Incidentally, the mountain referenced here was Mount Moriah, where the city of Jerusalem was later built. Jerusalem was the home of the temple, where God's presence dwelled with His people. Jesus' crucifixion occurred outside the gates of Jerusalem, where we now see even more clearly the Lord abundantly provided. The ram that God provided as a substitute for the death of Abraham's beloved son pointed to the substitutionary death that Jesus would die in the place of God's beloved children. God provided the substitutionary sacrifice of the ram in place of Abraham's son; He provided the substitutionary sacrifice of His own Son in our place.

The Passover story from Exodus 12 also points forward to penal substitution. As part of God's rescue plan for His people who were in captivity in Egypt, God told them to sacrifice an unblemished male sheep or goat and spread the animal's blood on their doorposts. If the angel of death saw the blood, he would pass over the home, sparing the lives of the firstborn. If the blood of the lamb was not sprinkled on the door, the firstborn son of that home was put to death. The unblemished animal served as a substitute for the firstborn son in each home. God rescued His people from Egyptian slavery that night by the blood of the sacrificed lamb. In doing so, He provided a multi-dimensional picture of a sacrifice that would serve as a substitute and provide the way of rescue to men who were captive to sin.

For centuries the Israelites offered bulls, goats, and lambs as a sacrifice to make atonement for their sin. These sacrifices were done under God's specific instructions to them. In God's economy, the blood of the lamb covered and displayed forgiveness for the sin of His people. Remember the Day of Atonement from chapter 8? The high priest would sacrifice one goat and then ceremoniously place his hands on the head of another goat, confessing the sins of the people. These goats were substitutes, punished in the place of God's people.

One of the most beloved passages in the Bible is found in chapter 53 of the book of Isaiah. Often referred to as the 'Servant Song,' it predicts a coming Messiah who will suffer for His people. Notice the language of both punishment and substitution in these verses:

Surely *he* has borne *our* griefs
    And carried *our* sorrows;
Yet we esteemed *him* stricken,
    Smitten by God, and afflicted.
But *he* was pierced for *our* transgressions;
    He was crushed for *our* iniquities;
Upon *him* was the chastisement that brought *us* peace,
    And with *his* wounds *we* are healed.
All *we* like sheep have gone astray;
    We have turned – every one – to his own way;
And the LORD has laid on *him*
    The iniquity of *us* all (Isa. 53:4-6).

Written hundreds of years before Jesus was born, this passage teaches that the coming servant will be crushed for the sins of His people, and that His chastisement will result in peace and healing for those for whom He is afflicted. This chapter shows the servant being stricken, smitten and afflicted by God Himself, who lays *on Him the iniquity of us all*. Go back and reread that passage looking at the pronouns. *He* bore…*our* griefs and *our* sorrows. *He* was pierced…for *our* transgressions. *He* was crushed…for *our* iniquities. By *His* wounds…*we* are healed. Clearly, *He* suffered by the hand of God – for *us*.

From the beginning the Old Testament is filled with historical events and prophecies that provide a runway to Jesus' grand work of penal substitution. (The examples offered are merely some of the many found in the Old Testament.) Understanding these examples in context of the cross helps us see that the Old Testament predicts *what* will happen to the Messiah. The New Testament explains *how* His death served as punishment from God for the sins of His people.

The Lamb of God

In the book of Mark, the author records a small word that gives great insight into the role of Jesus on the cross. Zebedee's sons James and John, both disciples of Jesus, asked Jesus for the honor of sitting on His left and His right in glory. Jesus responded, 'You do not know what you are asking. Are you able to drink the cup that I drink, or be baptized with the baptism with which I am baptized?' (Mark 10:35-38). A few chapters later in the Garden of Gethsemane, Jesus prays, 'Abba, Father, all things are possible for you. Remove this *cup* from me. Yet not what I will, but what you will' (Mark 14:36). What is this 'cup' that Jesus references? The one that He knows James and John would not ask to drink and that He Himself does not want to drink. It is the cup of God's wrath.

The Old Testament contains several descriptions of God's wrath being stored up in a cup. Psalm 75 ominously declares that at an appointed time God will judge the earth by pouring out His wrath. 'For in the hand of the Lord there is a cup with foaming wine, well mixed, and he pours out from it, and all the wicked of the earth shall drain it down to the dregs' (Ps. 75:8). Jeremiah also references this cup of wrath that belongs to the Lord for the 'wicked of the earth.' The ancient prophet said, 'Thus the LORD, the God of Israel, said to me: "Take from my hand and drink this cup of the wine of wrath, and make all the nations to whom I send you drink it. They shall drink and stagger and be crazed because of the sword that I am sending among them"' (Jer. 25:15-17). The next nine verses go on to list exactly who will taste the wine in the cup. The list starts with disobedient Jerusalem and the cities of Judah and continues with a comprehensive list of the nations at enmity with Yahweh. After listing most of the known world, included at the end, is 'all the kings of the north, far and near, one after another, all the kingdoms of the world that are on the face of the earth.' Through Jeremiah, God promises His wrath will be poured out, and the wicked people and nations of the earth will be punished for their sin.

There are other Old Testament references to God's cup of wrath, but what we see in the Old Testament is that the cup is full and waiting for the appointed time to be poured out in punishment for sin. And yet Jesus seems to be prepared to drink it, knowing fully how excruciating the drink will be. The passages above refer to the cup being full of the *wine* of wrath. The night before Jesus was crucified as He reclined at table with His disciples, He told them, 'This cup that is poured out for you is the new covenant in my blood' (Luke 22:20). The language translated here as 'for you' can also be translated as 'on your behalf' or 'in your place.' As God poured out the wine of his wrath on Jesus at the cross, Jesus poured out His blood for His people. The wine of wrath in God's cup has been replaced by the blood of Jesus, and a beautiful symbol is left for us at the Communion table to drink and remember.

After Jesus' conversation about the cup with James and John, the other disciples hear of it and are angry with the brothers. Jesus calls all of them together and says, '…whoever would be great among you must be your servant, and whoever would be first among you must be slave of all. For even the Son of Man came not to be served but to serve, *and to give his life as a ransom for many*' (Mark 10:43-45, emphasis mine). In the words of Jesus Himself, He will give His life in the place of those He came to serve. He knew His role was to take the punishment of sin in the place of others. Astonishingly, our God did not reveal Himself to mankind in order to be served by His creation, but instead He came to earth to serve His creation in the ultimate way.

Christ taking our place to suffer our punishment is an echo that reverberates throughout the New Testament. In Galatians, 'Christ redeemed us from the curse of the law by becoming a curse for us' (Gal. 3:13). In 2 Corinthians, 'For our sake he made him to be sin who knew no sin so that in him we might become the righteousness of God' (2 Cor. 5:21). Paul stands emphatically on the importance of understanding this fundamental theological truth. 'For I delivered to you as of first importance what I also received: that Christ died for our sins...' (1 Cor. 15:3).

Peter also writes about punishment and substitution: 'He himself bore our sins in his body on the tree, that we might die to sin and live to righteousness. By his wounds you have been healed' (1 Pet. 2:24). He repeats the theme, stating, 'For Christ also suffered once for sins, the righteous for the unrighteous, that he might bring us to God' (1 Pet. 3:18).

The book of Revelation, written to encourage churches to persevere to the end, shows us our reward in heaven is praising Jesus for His atoning work done on our behalf. The book refers to Jesus as the 'Lamb of God' twenty-seven times, clearly making the point that Christ has paid the penalty for our sins. We will worship Him forever for His sacrifice on our behalf.

John was given a vision of the end of time in heaven when a scroll with seven seals was ready to be opened. This scroll represents God's purposes for history. When the time came to open it, no one in heaven or on earth could be found who was worthy to open the scroll. At this, John began to weep loudly. He wept because at first no one was found worthy to bring about God's purposes for history. Imagine the despair this must have caused him, until dramatically he heard that 'the Lion of the tribe of Judah, the Root of David' could open it. But when he looked, he didn't see a lion but the 'Lamb who was slain!' The lamb who was slain is the lion of the tribe of Judah! And only He (Jesus) is the one worthy to open the scroll of God's eternal plan because He is the one who died to fulfill it. It is not merely Jesus' strength but His *sacrifice* that will elicit our praise throughout eternity.

Worthy are you to take the scroll
and to open its seals,

> for you were slain, and *by your blood you ransomed people*
> for God
> from every tribe and language and people and nation
> (Rev. 5:9).

At the cross we see God is the one actively bringing us to Himself. He provided the substitute of His own Son. Jesus said, 'I am the good shepherd. The good shepherd lays down his life for the sheep' (John 10:11). I would use the very words of Jesus Himself to answer the liberal theologians who suggest His death on the cross was abusive, not loving. 'Greater love has no one than this, that someone lay down his life for his friends' (John 15:13). Out of love, Jesus willingly was the sacrificial lamb of God who came to save His people from their sins.

High, Wide, Long and Deep

In our modern world – at least in the West – the concept of God's wrath may be met with some controversy, but the idea that He is loving is readily accepted. A nebulous, somewhat vague sense exists that if there is a God, He is a loving one. At the same time, God's love is defined not by the Bible but by subjective experience. This type of love creates a false foundation. As long as life is full of sunshine, we can all easily agree on the kindness of God, but of course we know life isn't always that way. The conversations I have had in just the last week with women reminds me of broken homes and wayward children, sickness and death, disappointment and loss. In the face of personal pain, how do we stand firmly on the foundation that God is love?

Our flimsy understanding of God's love needs a firmer foundation. Paul prayed for the Ephesian church to have the *power* to grasp how 'high and wide and long and deep is the love of Christ, and to know this love that surpasses knowledge' (Eph. 3:17-19, NIV). That prayer does not make sense if our understanding of God's love remains vague and uninformed. Why would we need *power* to understand love? Didn't Celine Dion already teach us to be 'ready to learn of the power of love'? If she articulates the depths of our understanding of what love is, we have given away something of infinite value and traded it in for something exceedingly inferior. Scripture thankfully reorients our thinking with a truthful definition of love. How do we know what God's love is like? John says, 'This is how we know what love is: Jesus Christ laid down his life for us' (1 John 3:16, NIV). Later he says it again in another way, 'This is how God showed his love among us: He sent his one and only Son into the world that we might live through him' (1 John 4:9).

If you want to grow in your knowledge of God's love – if you want to grasp how high and wide and long and deep it is – look at the cross. Gaze at Jesus, who left the glories and riches of heaven to come to earth as a lowly man, to die in your place. Look at His suffering. Consider the depths of your own personal sin and contrast it with the holiness of God, marveling at the fact that this God became man, suffering the indignation and shame of the cross. He bore all of the guilt that belonged to you and me, and yet He is the only one who deserved none of it. Jesus did not come to earth to be exalted by His creation, although that is what He deserved. He came into enemy lines to sacrifice Himself for those who hated Him. He laid down His life for those in active rebellion against Him. Paul knew of this irony. He said, 'God demonstrates his own love for us in this: While we were still sinners, Christ died for us' (Rom. 5:8, NIV). Jesus, pure light, the very radiance of God's glory, took on sinful flesh, and was pierced for us. We should have been objects of God's wrath, but instead He made us into objects of His mercy.

How do we reconcile God's love for us in the face of personal tragedy and difficulties in life? The Psalmist sang, 'Let the bones you have broken rejoice' (Ps. 51:8, NIV). How can we stand on the firm foundation that God is love? It is only with a dense, solid understanding of God's specific love for us in sending Jesus to suffer on our behalf that can we see this truth. If we are to face personal tragedy and still sing of God's glory, we must know of His love for us in sending Jesus to die on the cross.

Just as Beauty and the Beast is ultimately not about finding community or sacrificing for others, the gospel is not primarily about second tier issues. The cross is not just about fixing my needs or healing my brokenness, although those are benefits of a life in Christ. The cross is not only for the purpose of mending my difficult relationships or helping me find my purpose in life, though those are certain by-products of faith. The cross is about Jesus, full of love, coming to earth as a man, taking the punishment for my sin to suffer the death I deserve.

Why does Paul pray for the Ephesians to have the strength to understand this love? Because it is intense, full, deep and beautiful, and there is power in understanding God's specific love to us in the substitutionary death of Jesus. There is life to be found there. There is freedom from fear. There is victory over even our seemingly dark circumstances. 'Since he did not spare even his own Son but gave him up for us all, won't he also give us everything else?' (Rom. 8:32, NLT).

> Bearing shame and scoffing rude,
> In my place condemned He stood,
> Sealed my pardon with His blood:
> Hallelujah! What a Savior!
>
> Guilty, vile and helpless we;
> Spotless Lamb of God was He;
> Full atonement! Can it be?
> Hallelujah! What a Savior![11]

---

11   'Man of Sorrows! What a Name!', Philip P. Bliss.

QUESTIONS

PUNISHMENT IN OUR PLACE

While there were many things accomplished on the cross through Jesus' death, penal substitution–that Jesus took the punishment for our sin in our place–gets to the heart of what Jesus accomplished for sinners. The doctrine is foreshadowed in the Old Testament and explained in the New Testament.

1. How can a clear understanding of penal substitution show Sharon (p. 213) that God's love is more steadfast than her changing circumstances?

2. What about each of these theories is accurate? How are they each inadequate to explain penal substitution?
   Ransom theory
   Satisfaction theory
   Christus victor
   Exemplar

3. Penal Substitution was necessary because of God's wrath toward sin and because of His perfect justice. Explain each.

4. How does the Old Testament foreshadow the need for penal substitution?

5. Read Jeremiah 25:15-17 and Psalm 75:6-8. What is being stored in God's cup? Who is supposed to drink it? Now read Mark 10:35-38, Mark 14:35-36, and John 18:10-12. Who drank the cup? For whom?

6. Explain penal substitution and why it is central to understanding the cross.

7. How would you respond to a critic of penal substitution who says that it was not loving but it was cruel of God to require the death of Jesus, an innocent man, on our behalf?

Chapter 9

Purposes Accomplished:
A Display of His Glory

Tamela's marriage is in shambles. She looks at her peers and can only imagine what her life would be like if she and her husband had a healthy and loving relationship. He leads somewhat of a double life. Those at work and church think of him as the life of the party, but at home he is harsh and unkind. He has been looking at pornography for years and has no interest in stopping. There is little relationship left between the two of them. The difficulty at home has been weighing on her mental and spiritual wellbeing for some time now. At times she musters up a positive outlook to life, but it rarely stays longer than a few days. Overall, she cannot understand the purpose in her suffering. Having such a bad marriage feels so unfair to her. At a recent visit with her, she told you she doesn't know how much longer she can go on living like this.

As I approached the deadline for this book, my thoughtful husband Josh looked for ways to free up my time so I could write. Several evenings over the past few weeks he took our children out to dinner so I could stay home alone to work without distractions. The purpose in his taking them out was to give me the ability to work without the interruptions that can sometimes come from five energetic, inquisitive children. Our children may have seen the benefit to them (McDonalds on a school night? Yes!), but Josh did not take them to dinner merely for their sake. He was serving me while he met their need. The reason and the benefit were two separate things, although the action was the same for both. The reason was for me. The benefit was felt by them.

Often when we think of the atonement, we are quick to emphasize that through it, God provides salvation for sinners. Because people are the ones who benefit from this really good news, we tend to think of the cross chiefly in terms of what it accomplishes for us. But when we look at the cross, if we primarily see ourselves, we neglect to understand the full picture given in Scripture. We mistakenly think that we are both the reason for and the beneficiaries of the cross. Unsurprisingly, in our modern world of self-love, me time, and selfies, we tend to think the cross is only about me.

We do greatly (to put it mildly) benefit from the cross, but what is the primary reason given in Scripture for it? God's motivation in all things is the same: to bring Himself glory. Displaying His glory is the catalyst for all that He does both powerfully in the universe and quietly in our personal lives. His glory defines Him, and it enthralls us with a soul-satisfying knowledge (and therefore worship) of Him that nothing else can provide. God desires the weight of His glory to be known by His creation not out of narcissism, but because He knows nothing is more supremely beautiful and satisfying than Himself. And He wants the best for His beloved. As we know Him in dependency and joy, He is glorified and made known as supreme in the universe.

God's glory has been described as the sum total of all His attributes, the weight of the majesty of His being. His glory is His presence in full truth, and it encompasses the depths of His infinite beauty, along with the revelation of His character to His creation. So great is God's glory that finite, sinful man cannot survive the full weight of it. Remember Moses asked God to show him His glory, but God cautioned him that 'you cannot see my face, for man shall not see me and live' (Exod. 33:20). Recall from the last chapter that at the Day of Atonement the High Priest scattered incense from the burnt altar as soon as he entered the Most Holy Place so that he would not see the presence of God on his mercy seat. Paul did not say that 'all have sinned and fallen short of the *law* of God.' No, Paul said in our sin, 'we fall short of the *glory* of God' (Rom. 3:23). God's glory is the goal – both for us and for God. It is the overarching motivation for all He does. His glory is the end for which He created the world, the purpose of mankind, why He offers salvation to people, the foundation for the new covenant, and even the purpose of the law, among other things (Col. 1:16, Ps. 19:1-4, Isa. 43:7, Ezek. 20:44, Exod. 9:16, Ps. 106:8, Isa. 63:12-14, Ezek. 36:22-32, Isa. 42:21). Giving God glory is what we are to be doing 'whether we eat or we drink or whatever we do' (1 Cor. 10:31). Jesus – called the radiance of God's glory (Heb. 1:3) – even prayed before the cross that the Father would 'glorify the Son, that your Son may glorify you' (John 17:1). God's glory is the ultimate purpose of all things in, and even the existence of, the universe.

As the highest and most supreme being in the universe, God is always working for His own glory. The glorious God deserves our unending praise, and He is not bashful in seeking it. Some people mistakenly assume only a character flaw in God would cause Him to act on behalf of Himself, displaying His own glory and wanting others to praise Him for it. Rather, the opposite is true. God's *unblemished* character causes Him to act on behalf of His own name. The most supreme being in the universe should promote what is supremely good, not something of lesser worth. We can be assured then that God's glory motivates Him in all things, and it is therefore the overarching reason for Jesus' death on the cross.

Through an understanding of the primacy of God's glory, we can see that the atonement was primarily an act for God – in accordance with His will and to showcase His glory. For His own glory, God the Father is the one who ultimately put Jesus on the cross (Acts 2:23). The benefit of the cross is ours, but the reason was for God and His glory.

The obvious question we want to answer then is *how* was God glorified through the death of the Son? We are left again with the paradox of trying to understand how the death of Jesus brought glory to anyone, much less a sovereign and all-powerful God. At the cross, God's glory is on display as He manifests His full character to the world, He redeems His people in order for them to fully know and enjoy Him, and He defeats sin and evil.

Revelation of His Character

God's immutable character means He never changes. He always has been and will be the same as He is right now. But some aspects of God's character had not been as visible as others throughout Old Testament times. In a sense, they had been partially veiled prior to the cross. Always there, but not clearly observed. God's glory was on display at the cross as it illuminated who God is in ways that His people could from then on unquestionably understand.

When I was a toddler and my older brother Matt was in first grade, he rode the school bus each morning to school. Conveniently, the bus stopped just across the street from our house, so my mom kept an eye on my brother as he walked the short distance to catch his ride. But Matt had a first-grade habit of playing instead of planning, and he was often late to meet the bus. Superman was far more worthy of this six-year-old's time than learning to read. His habitual tardiness caused serious irritation for Mr. Ensign, the bus driver whose responsibility it was to get the children to school on time. One particularly memorable spring morning, the bus full of children arrived at its usual stop while my mom was still urging my brother to put down Batman and hurry to the bus stop. By the time my brother reached the bus, its doors had just closed, and the other neighborhood children were already finding their seats. I'm still not sure if Mr. Ensign did not see my brother or just wanted to teach him a lesson about timeliness, but he drove away toward the next stop while my brother was trying unsuccessfully to pry open the doors. My mom, watching this all unfold from our front door, saw my brother's superhero self-assurance take over, as he decided he could catch the bus whose wheels were taller than he was.

My mom, horrified, screamed hysterically for him to stop. My father, a man of decisive action, did not bother screaming. He had heard the commotion and had come out of his bedroom just in time to see Matt breathlessly running down the middle of the street dangerously close to oncoming traffic and a moving school bus that he was trying his hardest to get to stop. This would be a dilemma for any loving father. But unfortunately for everyone involved, the problem was compounded because my dad was in the middle of getting dressed.

In the following split second, my dad made a decision that would become folklore in our small hometown. Without hesitation or trousers, he darted out the front door running after my brother. By the time my dad caught up with Matt, the neighbors had come out of their homes, alerted to the unfolding drama by my mom's horrified screams and a nearly-naked grown man running down the street. Fortunately, before my brother caught up with the school bus, he was caught by my dad, solidifying my father's place as the greatest superhero of all time. My dad scooped my brother into his arms and carried him safely home. The neighbors were speechless as they watched my dad, far more concerned about his son than he was about the public appearance of his underwear.

Prior to this episode, my father had said things to my brother, older sister, and me like, 'I would do anything for you all.' We heard him say this, but we had not seen the lengths to which he was actually willing to go for us. After the episode of his running down the street in his underwear, we understood our father was willing to sacrifice his own good (and pride) if it meant protecting us. That spring morning's activities were a clear demonstration of this aspect of his character. He loved us and was willing to fiercely protect us, even at his own expense. The bus kids who had watched the episode out the back window probably wanted to make fun of my brother (and my dad), but they too saw the lengths our dad was willing to go to protect his son and decided it was wise to stay quiet. Along with his underwear, we all saw my dad's character on display in dramatic fashion.[1]

For centuries, God had been telling His people aspects of His character that they had not yet fully seen demonstrated. But it was at the cross that God's character was seen dramatically and clearly. All creation could see God's holiness, righteousness and justice, as well as His grace and love displayed in powerful clarity at the cross of Christ Jesus.

GOD'S HOLINESS

The holiness of God is perhaps His most defining characteristic, and while God ensured His people knew of His holiness in the Old Testament (Exod. 3:1-4, 17; Exod. 19:16-24; 2 Sam. 6:1-11), the cross provides a significantly clearer picture of it. God's holiness encompasses His moral purity, although there is a second use of the word in Scripture we must keep in mind. Holiness can also refer to being separate or intentionally set apart for God's use. God met Moses in a burning bush and even the ground around the bush was set apart as holy. That's why God told Moses to take off his shoes. He was standing on ground God was using to communicate to His servant (Exod. 3:1-6). Aaron was 'set apart' as the first high priest to make offerings to God and pronounce blessings from God (1 Chron. 23:13). His lineage became the priestly line, separate from the rest of the tribes of Israel to keep the worship of God according

---

1   In kindness toward my mom, I should add that she insists to this day my father was wearing pajama pants that morning.

to God's command. The center of the tabernacle was set apart as the Most Holy Place (Lev. 16) because that is where God's presence dwelled. No one could walk into that room nonchalantly and live. The presence of God and those things set apart for His worship were not to be treated casually. They were holy.

Unholy people cannot be in fellowship with a holy God. They have not been set apart for God's use, and they have no right to His morally pure presence. After all, God 'dwells in unapproachable light' (1 Tim. 6:16). Our sin keeps us separated. The only way a holy God and unholy people can exist together is if one becomes like the other. We know God will never compromise His holiness. He cannot; that would be a violation of His character. The cross then is the answer to the question of how a holy God can be reconciled to an unholy people. Through a perfectly holy mediator our sin can be paid for and we can be declared righteous. We can be set apart to be in the presence of God. God cannot sweep sin under a cosmic rug and pretend it does not matter. Nor can He accept an insufficient and inadequate payment for sin. The only acceptable form of payment for treason against a holy God is a perfectly holy substitute for us. Our guilt is punished in Jesus, and He transfers to us His righteousness so that we can be in communion with a holy God. Through this exchange of our sin for God's righteousness, God upholds His holy character by punishing sin and declaring His people holy in Christ. This does not compromise God's own holiness and righteousness. Instead, He removes our dirty sandals and gives us new metaphorical shoes so we can stand on His holy ground.

This great exchange – our sin for His righteousness – is what Paul boasts about to the Corinthians when he writes, 'For our sake he made him to be sin who knew no sin, so that in him we might become the righteousness of God' (2 Cor. 5:21). If you are in Christ, His righteousness now belongs to you. In theological terms, it has been imputed to you. This exchange rate is unbeatable. We trade in our sin and – in return – we get the perfect righteousness of the Lord Jesus. Cloaked in the righteousness of Christ, *we* are able to freely enter the most holy place. At the death of Jesus, the curtain in the temple separating the outer court from the Most Holy Place was torn in two from top to bottom, signifying that sin would no longer separate God's people from Him. Those who enter through Christ enter into the very presence of God (Matt. 27:51, Mark 15:38, Luke 23:45). Our perfect high priest has already made eternal atonement for us, and our sin no longer prevents us from approaching the holy God.

Paul tells us in Romans that Abraham's faith was credited to him as righteousness. Faith here is not a description of Abraham's character, but rather the means by which Abraham obtained the righteousness that would come from Christ. Abraham's faith was not 'close enough' to righteousness like if I owe you $20 but only have $18 and you tell me not to worry about the rest. We cannot say that Abraham was a faithful man, and so God honored him with full righteousness. Abraham was a sinner, but God gave him the righteousness that belonged to Jesus because he believed God's promise. And for those who believe in Christ, what is true for Abraham is true for us. After all, Paul wrote later, 'And to the one who does not work but believes in him..., his faith is counted as righteousness' (Rom. 4:5). Praise God! '...by the one man's obedience the many will be made righteous' (Rom. 5:19). Our imputed righteousness allows us to be in fellowship with the holy God.

The fact that God sent His only Son to become sin and transfer His righteousness to us so that we can be in fellowship with Him shows us the magnitude of the holiness of God. God Himself was willing to suffer to uphold His character while saving us.

GOD'S RIGHTEOUSNESS AND JUSTICE

Because of God's holiness, He demands punishment for sin. This is another aspect of God's character that was clearly seen at the cross. Scripture refers to His demand for moral perfection as His righteousness and justice. These English words are how we generally translate the concept that God does not answer to any other authority for a code of conduct or moral standard. He does not answer to any other standard because He is the very definition of righteousness. No one and no thing is more morally pure than He is.

Paul explained to the Romans that '[Jesus' death] was to show God's righteousness, because in his divine forbearance he had passed over former sins' (Rom. 3:25). In what sense had former sins been passed over prior to the cross? In the Old Testament, God showed a tremendous patience toward His sinful people. In scene after scene of the Old Testament, God did not deal with sin as it deserved. His people both corporately and individually disobeyed God, and yet God continued to spare them. At times His wrath would burn hot, and He would send a plague, famine, or neighboring army to punish the people for their wickedness, but the problem of sin was not comprehensively addressed on the scale which it warranted. Their sins were often (but not always) punished, but their Sin was not. 'The times of ignorance God overlooked' is how Paul explained God's patience in addressing sin (Acts 17:30). In His mercy, God continued to allow His sinful people to live. Even the prophet Micah laments the wickedness of the people and asks the legitimate question, 'Who is a God like you, pardoning iniquity and passing over transgression…?' (Micah 7:18). In praise the Psalmist repeats this truth about God, 'He does not deal with us according to our sins, nor repay us according to our iniquities' (Ps. 103:10). These questions highlight God's mercy, but how can a God who doesn't punish sin be just?

After David's infidelity with Bathsheba and his wickedness toward her husband Uriah the Hittite, the prophet Nathan rebuked King David, who in turn confessed his sin before the Lord. And then astonishingly Nathan responds, 'The LORD also has put away your sin; you shall not die' (2 Sam. 12:9-13). A first-time reader of this passage should gasp. David took another man's wife and then had that man killed in battle, and the Lord just 'put away' his sin? Where is the justice in that for Uriah, or even Bathsheba? How can a good God not punish wickedness? One might be tempted to think God could just look away and disregard sin as irrelevant or unimportant whenever He wanted to, but that would mean He is unjust and does not treat sin as it deserves. The sinner would surely appreciate such mercy, but what about the victim? Where is the justice for the innocent?

God could not simply 'put away' sin and maintain His justice at the same time. He could not be a God of righteousness without comprehensively addressing the problem of sin. His patience toward sinners should not be mistaken for apathy toward sin. Back to what Paul wrote to the Romans: '[Jesus' death] was to show God's righteousness, because in his divine forbearance he had passed over former sins.' Jesus' death on the cross displayed God's perfect righteousness and justice. The sin, like David's, that had been passed over for centuries was finally given the knock-out blow it deserved. All the sins for all God's children for all time were laid on Jesus when He died, and all the world could see the glory of God's righteous character on display as His wrath poured out for this sin.

The other way in which God's righteousness and justice are clearly seen in the cross is by observing the lengths that God went to maintain this part of His character. The Father was willing to send His only Son into the world to die a humiliating death in order to punish sin in the way His justice required. For God to be a righteous and just God, sin could not be ignored. It had to be confronted. And punished. Jesus Himself was willing to suffer and die – even taking the punishment on Himself – in order to address sin in a way that upheld the character of God.

In recounting God's faithfulness to generations, Asaph said of God, 'He restrained his anger often and did not stir up all his wrath' (Ps. 78:38). It is a myth that the God of the Old Testament is wrathful and angry, but the God of the New Testament is not. Just like it's a myth that the God of the New Testament is loving, but the God of the Old Testament is not. In episode after episode, God shows Himself incredibly patient with, and merciful to, sinners for generations and generations. God waited to deal with sin as it deserved. At the cross, we see God's glorious justice enacted toward sin as the God-man Jesus bore the punishment for the sins of His people.

Do you ever consider God's justice when you take account of your own life? Do your trials ever seem 'unfair?' We can be confident that a God who goes to such great lengths to protect His justice is a God who is always acting in a just and right manner. He does not send anything to us in the form of a trial that is not just. We cannot complain that our circumstances are unfair when we look at the cross. Jesus is the only person in history who was punished when He deserved none. Would you reconsider your accusation against God as being unfair for the trial you find yourself in? Whatever the current trial you are experiencing, it has been designed by a just God to bring about our growth in righteousness–to make us more like Christ.

GOD'S LOVE

God never acts in an unfair manner. Instead, God delights in showcasing His steadfast love for His people. As early as Genesis, God's love was described as steadfast toward Joseph (Gen. 39:21). His love is how He introduced Himself to Moses in Exodus (Exod. 34:6). The prophets knew of God's disdain for sin, and so they praised God for His surprisingly steadfast love for His sinful people (Lam. 3:22-23). The psalmists, in awe and worship of God because of it, regularly wrote about God's love with praise and thanksgiving. God's steadfast love endures forever (Ps. 118, Ps. 136).

The cross provides the answer to the problem of how a holy God can uphold His justice while also showing love and forgiveness to His people. One might be tempted to think these two aspects of His character – His perfect justice and love – run parallel to each other. But it was at the cross where the Father's justice and love most gloriously met. If God's nature had only been one of holiness, justice, and righteousness, there would have been a need for the cross but no *willingness* to endure it. But in His steadfast and great love for His people, He was willing to suffer on their behalf. We see how the Psalmist could foretell, 'Steadfast love and faithfulness meet; righteousness and peace kiss each other' (Ps. 85:10).

The evidence for God's love for sinners can be seen especially in our unworthiness to receive such a sacrificial gift. Paul wrote in Romans, 'One will scarcely die for a righteous person – though perhaps for a good person one would dare even to die' (Rom. 5:7). We were neither righteous nor good when God enacted His rescue plan for sinners. When God sent Jesus into the world to die on our behalf, we were in outright rebellion against God. 'God shows his love for us in that while we were still sinners, Christ died for us' (Rom. 5:8). Do you see how God says He demonstrates His love for us? It is our unworthiness to receive the gift of Christ's death that magnifies God's love for us.

I'm a sucker for home renovation shows. I appreciate (and sometimes covet) a designer's ability to transform an ordinary looking home into magazine-worthy beauty. But I equally love the backstory of the person whose home is being renovated. The war vet who lost his ability to provide for his family because of his sacrifice to his country. Or the exhausted homeschool mom who has adopted special needs children. We celebrate these people as *worthy* of the gift they will receive. In doing so, we magnify the one receiving the gift. If we want to magnify the giver, we need to look for a story where a gift is given to one who is unworthy of receiving it.

Recent news stories showed a powerful image from a courtroom proceeding in Dallas, Texas. An innocent man had been murdered by a policewoman who had mistakenly thought the man was in her apartment. The victim's brother, while grieving the unnecessary and painful death of his loved one, publicly offered the accused full forgiveness and even remarkably asked the judge for permission to give the accused a hug. I watched the video of that powerful embrace multiple times, never with a dry eye. The focus of our attention shifts in that episode from the undeserving cop who received forgiveness to the remarkable action of the one who issued it. His character (and his belief that Jesus calls us to forgive others as we have been forgiven) captivated my attention because she was undeserving of his gift of forgiveness.

The story of Hosea and Gomer provides another captivating example of one's unworthiness in comparison to the gift offered. Hosea was one of God's highly-esteemed prophets. Gomer was akin to the town prostitute. And yet God commanded Hosea to take Gomer as his bride. Hosea obeyed God, but instead of answering his kindness with faithfulness, Gomer wandered. Again, Hosea called her away from the arms of another lover and back to fidelity with himself. She was undeserving of his love, and yet he was faithful to give it. What do we make of a man like Hosea? Is he an anomaly in Scripture? Or is he one of many examples that show this pattern of undeserved love? The cowardly liar Abraham didn't deserve the blessings God bestowed on him. The cheating Jacob didn't deserve to be the father of Israel. Joseph's wicked brothers didn't deserve his forgiveness and provision. The murderer Moses didn't deserve to have such a highly esteemed position before God. The grumbling people of Israel who preferred to return to slavery didn't deserve the manna God provided every day. I could continue. Page after page of Scripture shows one disproportionate relationship after another, a generous gift offered to an unseemly recipient.

Of all those pictures of one receiving a gift they did not deserve, none illustrates the point more clearly than the cross where Jesus died for sinners. He did not die for the lovely. He did not come for those who had earned His affection. He came to rescue the vilest of sinners. He came to pursue in love those who were in an attempted coup against Him. He is the handsome prince who desires to husband the ugly whore. At the cross we see God's love for His people magnified because He died for those who did not deserve it.

Isn't one of the deepest desires in all of our lives to be fully known and still fully loved? God is fully aware of who we are in our sin, and yet He offers to us His sacrificial, bottomless, unconditional love. As our maker, He knows us intimately. He knows things about us we have not yet discovered for ourselves. And yet His love for us has no time limit and no end. Nothing can cause His love to weaken or fray or ever fall away. 'Who shall separate us from the love of Christ? Shall tribulation, or distress, or persecution, or famine, or nakedness, or danger, or sword?' (Rom. 8:35). Paul asks the question and then answers it, 'I am sure that neither death nor life, nor angels nor rulers, nor things present nor things to come, nor powers, nor height nor depth, nor anything else in all creation, will be able to separate us from the love of God in Christ Jesus our Lord' (Rom. 8:38-39). Because of the cross of Christ, we can see clearly God's vast and endless love for His people.

GOD'S GRACE

In Romans, Paul calls God both the 'just and the justifier of the one who has faith in Jesus' (Rom. 3:26). He was the one offended, and yet remarkably He is the one who paid the penalty for the offense. In the often-used legal analogy, God was the judge who rendered a verdict against the guilty and ordered their punishment, but then He was also the one who took the place of the condemned and accepted the punishment on their behalf.

Sin was against God. God's righteousness demanded a penalty for it. God both enacted and received the punishment for man's sin. God declares people are justified by the work of His own Son. All of this work begins and ends with God. And because He is the author and executer of this work, there is no room for boasting by men. There is no place for pride at the foot of the cross – only the humble recognition that we contributed nothing. Every part of salvation was designed by God and achieved through Jesus. The cross is 100% grace. Paul writes, 'For by grace you have been saved through faith. And this is not your own doing; it is the gift of God, not a result of works, so that no one may boast' (Eph. 2:8-9). We do not deserve salvation, and we have not done any of the work required to earn it. All glory goes to God as the cross is all by His grace.

The cross – beautifully, ruggedly, painfully – displayed the magnificent character of God in ways that had not been seen clearly prior to the cross. He is holy. He is just and righteous. He is full of steadfast love and grace.

Restoration of the Relationship

There is another way the cross of Christ glorifies God, and perhaps surprisingly to you it has a lot to do with our joy. We know that through Christ's obedience to the Father at the cross, He forged a path for us to be reconciled to our Creator, the One whose image we bear. 'Christ died…that he might bring us back to God' (1 Pet. 3:18). This reconciliation of individual men and women to God is the greatest gift we can ever receive.

How do *you* define what makes the good news of the Gospel so good? Is the good news to you primarily that you can be saved from eternal punishment? All people have an interest in avoiding pain; it certainly does not take a supernaturally changed heart to want to avoid misery. Or is the good news of the Gospel that you get God? Does your heart long for the deep, abiding, unfailing joy that comes from knowing the One whose image you bear? Those in Christ don't merely avoid hell; they get the deepest, most satisfying, and longest-lasting, supernatural joy a human being can know. They get God Himself. Only through Jesus can we know God, and in the presence of God is a joy that cannot be surpassed by any other thing. The Psalmist wrote, '…in your presence there is fullness of joy; at your right hand are pleasures forevermore' (Ps. 16:11).

Experiencing satisfaction from knowing God is good for us, but how does our joy bring God glory? Did Jesus really suffer and die for our joy? The answer is that we were made to enjoy Him, and we bring Him glory as we fulfill the purpose for which He made us. Our purpose is to know God and enjoy Him forever. Seeing and savoring His glory will bring us a deep and soul-satisfying enjoyment that lasts for all eternity. While our sin prevents us from fully seeing His glory now, one day we will see Him face-to-face and live.

John Piper wrote, '…we were made to experience full and lasting happiness from seeing and savoring the glory of God. If our best joy comes from something less, we are idolaters and God is dishonored. He created us in such a way that his glory is displayed through our joy in it. The gospel of Christ is the good news that at the cost of his Son's life, God has done everything necessary to enthrall us with what will make us eternally and ever-increasingly happy, namely, himself.'[2] God is glorified in our eternal and full enjoyment of Him. He made us not just to know Him, but to *enjoy* Him.

How do you respond to the idea that getting God and His full, unmediated glory will be your greatest reward and fullest delight? Does this knowledge have any effect on your life on earth today?

---

2   John Piper, *Fifty Reasons Why Jesus Came to Die* (Wheaton, IL: Crossway, 2006), p. 63.

Are you enjoying God day-to-day? Do you live as if this life were all there is, spending significant amounts of time and resources making your life here as comfortable and happy as possible? Consider for a moment what your goals are in life – are they all financial? Status-related? Have you even thought about how to strategically spend your time during the decades you are likely given on this earth? Are you pointing others to the eternally satisfying joy that comes from God? The good news of the Gospel is that those who are in Christ get God Himself, and there is no other deeper source of joy than that. This good news is meant to be shared. It is meant to be embraced. It is meant for God's glory to be displayed in our eternal enjoyment of Him.

Defeat of Evil

Finally, the cross marvelously revealed God's glory as Jesus defeated sin and evil. Remember back in the Garden of Eden when sin was first introduced to God's good world? Adam and Eve chose to eat the forbidden fruit from the tree of the knowledge of good and evil, setting into motion a deluge of evil into the world. The cross began to undo the effects of evil that had been permeating creation ever since Genesis 3.

Adam ate from the forbidden tree and brought death to the world. Jesus hung on a tree, and by doing so brought life to all who would believe. Adam's sin at the tree led to shame. At Jesus' tree, He took away our sin and shame. God showed mercy to Adam and clothed His nakedness. Jesus, while showing mercy at the cross, was stripped naked. Adam disobeyed God at the tree. Jesus fully obeyed His Father, even to the point of death on the tree. What Adam brought into the world, Jesus banished at the cross.

As stated before, God could not simply ignore man's defiance of His authority and rejection of His majesty; sin is a direct attack on God's glory. God hates sin and all evildoers (Ps. 5:4-6). He takes 'vengeance on his adversaries and keeps wrath for his enemies'

(Nahum 1:2). The punishment He promised for sin has been unambiguous ever since He first spoke to Adam, promising death for disobedience. Adam knew his transgression would cause him to 'surely die' (Gen. 2:17). God repeated this punishment to Ezekiel: 'The soul who sins shall die' (Ezek. 18:4). His wrath toward sinners is a repeated chorus throughout both the Old and New Testaments (Exod. 32:11; 2 Kings 22:17; 2 Chron. 34:25, 36:16; Ezra 10:14; Ps. 78:59; Jer. 7:20, 42:18; Ezek. 22:31; Rom. 1:18, 5:9, 13:4; Eph. 2:3, 5:6; Col. 3:6). Even if man brushes off sin as a mistake, God clearly takes it seriously. God's consistent stance against sin shows up on page after page of Scripture.

The cross was God's full-frontal attack on sin and evil.

But to be certain, as Jesus hung dying on the cross, it *looked* like evil had defeated what was good. For a time, it appeared that the maker of the universe was going to succumb to a wooden cross and an evil plot against Him. And yet what was visible was not reality. John Stott wrote, 'Crushed by the ruthless power of Rome, he was himself crushing the serpent's head (Gen. 3:15). The victim was the victor, and the cross is still the throne from which he rules the world.'[3]

His war on sin was more than individual battles in the lives of His people. At a cosmic level, He defeated evil at the cross. '[He] gave himself for our sins to deliver us from the present evil age' (Gal. 1:4). While somewhat out of vogue in some parts of the modern world, Satan is a real being, and he rules over dark spiritual evil. He has had real power in this world, and you need to look no further than your own life for proof: 'You once walked, following the course of this world, following the prince of the power of the air, the spirit that is now at work in the sons of disobedience' (Eph. 2:2).

Jesus' death on the cross broke the bondage to sin so that those who are in Christ know true freedom. That's what delivery from

---

3   Stott, *The Cross of Christ*, p. 228.

'the present evil age' means. Those who are in Christ are no longer following a defeated master, but they are following the risen, conquering, serpent-crushing King.

Those who follow this King, follow Him into life. Jesus is the first to be resurrected from the dead. But all those in Christ will one day follow Him out of their graves and into the new creation. Paul explains this will happen when 'the end will come,' and when Jesus will defeat the last enemy: death (1 Cor. 24-26, NIV). Death has always been the result of man's sin. There has been no remedy from it and no inoculation to prevent it from coming for all of us. But at the cross Jesus overturned the power of death, and when He comes again, death will be swallowed up forever. 'When the perishable has been clothed with the imperishable, and the mortal with immortality, then the saying that is written will come true: 'Death has been swallowed up in victory' (1 Cor. 15:54, NIV). With this truth in mind, we no longer have to fear death. We can instead sing confidently with Hosea, 'Where, O death is your victory? Where, O death, is your sting?' (1 Cor. 15:55, Hosea 13:14, NIV).

DEBT FREE AND VICTORIOUS

There are two significant ways in which Jesus defeated sin and overcame evil at the cross. One is that our sin, as a violation of God's law, had us in debt to God. At the cross, God frees us from our debt and destroys all records of it. Satan's greatest weapon against us had been his accusation to God that His people are guilty. By paying the debt that we owed, Jesus liberated us from this guilt – and therefore Satan's power. The debt we owed to God because of our sin was nailed to the cross. 'You, who were dead in your trespasses and the uncircumcision of your flesh, God made alive together with him, having forgiven us all our trespasses, by canceling the record of debt that stood against us with its legal demands. This he set aside, nailing it to the cross.' (Col. 2:13-14).

The second way Jesus defeated evil at the cross was by resisting the devil's temptations to get Him to sin. Remember that even one 'small' act of sin by Jesus would have ruined God's rescue plan for sinners. Jesus put those efforts by Satan to shame by rebuffing every temptation to disobey the will of the Father. He disarmed the rulers and authorities and put them to open shame, by triumphing over them in him. (Col. 2:15) How foolish Satan appeared when he threw all his power behind derailing God's mission, only to fail miserably. Jesus made a public spectacle of Satan and his army's vast efforts to thwart His divine mission, and He triumphed over them, even as He hung on a cross. What appeared to be weakness was actually God's divine plan to overthrow Satan.

At the Great Commission Jesus made it clear that He has all authority now. Satan has no authority over those who are in Christ. As a result, we can now 'walk in a manner worthy of the Lord, fully pleasing to him, bearing fruit in every good work and increasing in the knowledge of God.' The reason for this life worthy of the Lord is that we are no longer under the domain of darkness. We have been delivered from it and transferred to a new realm – the kingdom of the beloved Son. (Col. 1:10-14).

This victorious God who was able to defeat every evil power is the God who offers Himself freely to you. Our anthem in life should therefore be: 'If God is for us, who can be against us?' (Rom. 8:31). There is no person, no power, no ruler, no authority who is stronger than our God. And our God offers you safety and security under His wing of protection. Because of this truth, we can live victorious and fearless lives for His glory. We do not have to fear evil. We do not have to fear Satan or any of his minions. We are on the side of the victorious King, the One who made a spectacle of Satan's power.

And yet, there are times we face real evil in this world. Tragic things happen to us and to our families, and it may feel at times as though darkness is winning. It might seem as though we may be the ones who succumb to the evil in this world. We may feel as though we are drowning in the consequences of sin – our own or someone else's. This God who knows the full extent of evil also promises to be our help in times of need (Ps. 46:1). The Psalms are full of promises of His protection. In Psalm 91, He calls Himself our shelter. Our fortress. These are strong and powerful images of protection against an enemy who has launched an attack. In the same Psalm He promises, 'under his wings you will find refuge.' By His side near His bosom, He offers us the security of His protection. He offers us nearness to Himself.

These are life-giving words in Psalm 91 from God to those in need:

> Because he holds fast to me in love, I will deliver him;
> I will protect him, because he knows my name.
> When he calls to me, I will answer him;
>> I will be with him in trouble;
>> I will rescue him and honor him.
> With long life I will satisfy him
>> And show him my salvation (Ps. 91:14-16).

Our God has defeated evil and every obstacle that stands in the way of a relationship with you. And He has done so for His name's sake. For His glory, hold fast to Him in love.

Glory at the Cross

God's glory is bound up in the person and work of Christ. Consider how many times God's glory is linked directly with Christ, even from the beginning of His life. The Magnificat, Mary's beautiful song of praise to God for the privilege of being the mother of the Messiah, begins, 'My soul glorifies the Lord and my spirit rejoices in God my Savior' (Luke 1:46-47, NIV). When the angels announced the birth of Jesus to the shepherds tending their flocks, they exclaimed, 'Glory to God in the highest!' (Luke 2:14). Jesus' prayer to the Father just hours before the crucifixion was that the Father would receive glory from it (John 17:1). When the apostles scattered to preach about the crucified and risen Lord Jesus, they did it 'for the sake of his name' (Rom. 1:5, 3 John 7). God's glory is shown through the life and death of His Son. Not only is the person of Jesus 'the radiance of God's glory and the exact imprint of his nature' (Heb. 1:3) but His work – particularly His atoning death – is a magnificent display of God's character, His desire for His people to know and enjoy Him, and His victory over evil and sin.

> See, from His head, His hands, His feet
> Sorrow and love flow mingled down
> Did e'er such love and Sorrow meet
> Or thorns compose so rich a crown.
>
> Were the whole realm of nature mine
> That were an offering far too small.
> Love so amazing, so divine
> Demands my soul, my life, my all.[4]

---

4   'When I Survey the Wondrous Cross', Isaac Watts, (Riegger).

QUESTIONS

PURPOSES ACCOMPLISHED

It was the will of God for Jesus to suffer and die on the cross. This atonement displayed God's glory. For in it, God revealed His character, redeemed His people to know and enjoy Him, and defeated sin and evil.

1. How can gazing at the cross change Tamela's (p. 189) outlook on life?

2. When we think of the atonement, we are sometimes too quick to describe it only in terms of our benefit: that God provides salvation for sinners. Why might leaving out the display of God's glory cause a distortion in our view of the cross?

3. What is God's glory? How is our sin an attack on His glory?

4. Written hundreds of years before the cross, Psalm 85 declares, 'Steadfast love and faithfulness meet; righteousness and peace kiss each other.' How could the Psalmist write with confidence of a God who was both loving and righteous? How did the cross most fully display God's character?

5. Read Romans 3:25. In what sense had God passed over sins?

6. Another aspect of God's character that was clearly seen on the cross was His grace. Read Romans 3:26-27. Why is the fact that God is both the just and the justifier evidence of this grace?

7. Another aspect of God's character on display is found in the familiar verse John 3:16. How is God's love most profoundly seen at the cross?

8. How does our joy in God bring Him glory and what does the cross have to do with it?

9. How does the victory of the cross bring God glory?

Chapter 10

Perfect Ending:
Union With Christ

All of Stephanie's closest friends have gotten married and are having children. She wants to be happy for them, but she also wants to know when marriage and children will happen for her. She has grown increasingly insecure at church sitting alone and feels awkward when her friends talk about their pregnancies and their children. She heard the pastor say that her identity should be in Christ, not in worldly things, but she doesn't know what that means for her.

Of all the truths we have studied about Christ, there is one that is so profoundly beautiful and practically helpful that we should speak of it on a daily basis. We should sing about it in our worship songs, remind each other about it in our conversations, and preach it powerfully from our pulpits. And yet regrettably, it is often sidelined. At best, it is assumed. At worst, ignored. It is a doctrine far too long neglected and left in the upper attic of the ivory towers of theology. It is clearly present in Scripture and is one of the most practical doctrines for Christians who face the ordinary struggles of life, but it has not permeated the modern church with vigor.

A.W. Pink wrote, 'The subject of spiritual union is the most important, the most profound, and...the most blessed of any that is set forth in the sacred Scripture. Yet, sad to say, there is hardly any that is now more generally neglected.'[1] He wrote those words in 1971, and yet nearly fifty years later, most Christians today still could not articulate what it means to be united with Christ and why it is of any relevance to their lives at all. Martin Lloyd Jones called it the 'greatest and most marvelous of all the Christian doctrines, one of the most glorious beyond any question at all.' And Charles Spurgeon once said, 'There is no joy in this world like union with Christ. The more we can feel it, the happier we are.'

These and many other brilliant theologians have argued that Christians are malnourished on this crucial topic that (ironically) saturates the New Testament. To be fair, several books have been written on this topic in the last few years, but seemingly the truth of this doctrine has not yet trickled into mainstream modern Christian conversation. For proof, think about how you refer to those who have been converted. You might say someone is following Jesus, or is a believer, or say they have been born again. You probably also use the term Christian. These are all fine descriptors, but they are not the primary ways the early Christians thought of themselves. Paul uses the phrase 'in Christ' (or 'in him') in his letters around 165 times. By contrast, 'Christian' is only found three times, and it seems likely that term was initially one of derision rather than affection. The term 'in Christ' captures the intimate relationship between the believer and God through Christ in a way that is missed when we simply say some has faith or believes.

Inherent in the term 'in Christ' is the work that Christ has done to secure this personal relationship and the benefits to the believer

---

1   A.W. Pink, *Spiritual Union and Communion* (Grand Rapids, MI: Baker, 1971), p. 7.

because of it. The doctrine of the Union with Christ teaches us that we are woven so tightly to Jesus that what is true for Him is now true for us. We are in Him, and He is in us. At conversion we are not just saved from hell, or even merely made right with God, but we are united to our Savior in an inseparable manner. The Holy Spirit unites us to Jesus so that our earthly lives are one with His heavenly life with God. The by-product of this union is that our identity is joined to His. And because of this newfound intimacy, we are entitled to experience personally all the success of Christ. All the acceptance that God showed Jesus at His baptism and at the transfiguration. All the accomplishments of Christ at the cross. All the joy and glory that He now knows as He rules over the cosmos and is seated at the right hand of His Father. All the fullness and all the resources found in Christ are ours, when we are joined with Him at our conversion.

This doctrine is foundational to both our salvation and our sanctification, and it is essential to the deepest joys we will know in this life and the next. John Piper said, 'When this is fully understood, nothing is greater experientially, and nothing is greater theologically. You cannot experience anything greater than the fullness of union with Christ.'[2] Being in Christ is the whole point of the gospel. Indeed, union with Christ is the message of hope we hold out to the world. In Christ we are offered the deepest joys and the greatest fulfilment possible to man. It shouldn't surprise us then that John Calvin ranked Union with Christ at 'the highest degree of importance.'[3]

Where He Goes, I Go
In April 1970, people all over the world were enthralled with the story of NASA's Apollo 13 mission to land on the moon. Two days into the flight and approximately 205,000 miles from Earth,

---

2   John Piper, sermon, 2014 Desiring God conference, Feb 3, 2014.

3   Calvin, *Institutes*, 737 (3.11.10).

an oxygen tank onboard exploded during a routine check of the systems, and it severely damaged the ability of the crew to command the spacecraft. For the next four days dozens of engineers, scientists, astronauts, and mathematicians carefully calculated how to get that crippled spacecraft with waning oxygen levels and battery power safely back to Earth. The families and friends of the three astronauts on board cared deeply about the destiny of the spacecraft because of who was inside it. The fate of their loved ones was tied up with the fate of that shuttle. Where that shuttle went, so went the people in it.

Union with Christ means just that. We are in Him, and our life depends on Him, in the way the astronauts were dependent on the fate of the shuttle. Paul uses the term 'in Christ' (or, 'in Him,' 'in whom,' etc.) to describe our union with Christ at every step of His life and work. A few significant examples: we have been crucified with Christ (Rom. 6:6), raised with Him (Rom. 6:5), glorified with Him (Rom. 8:17), able to reign with Him (2 Tim. 2:12), made alive in Him (Col. 2:13), hidden with Him (Col. 3:3), are one flesh with Him (Eph. 5:31-32), part of His body, (1 Cor. 12:27) and co-heirs with Him (Rom. 8:17). Paul is communicating something to us as he speaks of both our suffering with Christ and our exaltation with Him. He is telling us our destiny is tied up with Christ in a relationship that is never to be broken or frayed. The relationship between Christ and the believer is so connected that He not only says we are in Him but that He is also in us. Someone who is in Christ is there to stay.

BELOVED DAUGHTER

Jesus explained to His disciples that their relationship with Him is rooted in His relationship with God the Father. He is the Son of God, and now that we are in Him, we have become children of God. Children have rights and privileges that are not available to those outside the family. Paul wrote in Romans, '…if children, then heirs – heirs of God and fellow heirs with Christ, provided we suffer with him in order that we may also be glorified with him' (Rom. 8:17). Because of our union with Christ, whatever is His, is ours. His suffering is ours. His victory is ours. His glory is ours. All because He shares His Sonship with us. He doesn't do so as a resentful sibling who is begrudgingly forced to divvy up an inheritance. He shares all that He has abundantly with us.

He has this union in mind when He prays to the Father just hours before His crucifixion. He prays for the disciples' unity to result from His unity with the Father: 'I in them and you in me, that they may become perfectly one, so that the world may know that you sent me and loved them even as you loved me' (John 17:23). That is a theological feast of a verse, but certainly the main course is that the Father loves those in Christ with the same love that He has for the Son. Let that sink in: 'You loved them even as you loved me,' Jesus says. Our intimate communion with Christ brings us into intimate communion with the Father. Recall at Jesus' baptism, the Father speaks from heaven, 'This is my beloved Son, with whom I am well pleased' (Matt. 3:17). The parable of the talents predicts a similarly pleased Father who welcomes His servant into the 'joy of the master' with the words, 'Well done good and faithful servant' (Matt. 25:23). Because you have been grafted into Christ, God the Father now loves you in the same way that He loves Jesus. This love is endless. It has existed for all eternity and will continue for all eternity. It is a patient and kind love, always seeking the best, never waning or fading. It is all we'll ever need. If you are in Christ, you will one day hear, 'This is my beloved daughter, with whom I am well pleased.'

Not Just a Fan

I admire some musicians but God has not gifted me with any musical ability, so I am definitely not *in* any band. (My family won't even let me sing in the car.) I am a fan of certain sports teams, but God gifted me with even less athletic ability, so you definitely don't want me on your team. Being a fan is clearly different than being 'in.' Viewing a game as a spectator is different from watching as a competitor. Participation is more significant than admiration. We too often think of ourselves as following Christ instead of understanding that we have the privilege of being in Christ. Our relationship to Him is deeper than being even the most devoted fan.

Is this merely semantics–similar to the difference between going on a holiday or going on vacation? Regardless of how you describe it, you end up at the same place. No, neglecting to understand this Biblical teaching has the potential for us to undermine the person of Christ and overemphasize man. We must be careful to intentionally keep Christ at the center of our relationship and not the mere means to an end. Sinclair Ferguson wrote, 'If [being in Christ] is not the overwhelmingly dominant way in which we think about ourselves, we are not thinking with the renewed mind of the gospel. But in addition, without this perspective it is highly likely that we will have a tendency to separate Christ from his benefits and abstract those benefits from him...as though we possessed them in ourselves.'[4]

The danger in not understanding what it means that we are in Christ is that we may separate who Jesus is from what He has done for us. We run the risk of wanting just what appeals most to us, as if we are going through a buffet line. We don't just select the easy parts of salvation and the benefits that come from it. At our conversion, we get the whole Christ. Not part of Him. Not just the benefits He offers. We get *Him*–relationship with Him and the Father! All the benefits are subservient to and flow from the relationship.

To be 'in Christ' is more significant than to be a mere fan, or even a disciple. How can we devotedly follow Him? How can we truly obey? How can we admire Him as we ought? A follower can

---

4   Sinclair Ferguson, *The Whole Christ: Legalism, Antinomianism and Gospel Assurance* (Wheaton, IL: Crossway, 2016), p. 45.

stop following. A fan can switch allegiances. It is only in our unity with Christ that we can live the Christian life. He must be at the center.

Are You 'In'?

The language of being 'in' is not a sentimental idea or a clever analogy, similar to how we may casually say someone has fallen 'in' love. Rather, Scripture uses this term to communicate something concrete about our relationship with Jesus. If some people are in Christ, many people are also 'out.' The lines have been drawn and we are all on one side or the other.

Being in Christ means I am no longer in Adam. Being made alive *in Christ* only happens when we repent of our sins and believe in Jesus. This transition by the power of the Holy Spirit means that God comes in and closes up your home in the slums of Adam's neighborhood and gives you the keys to a spiritual mansion in a new kingdom where Christ reigns. At your conversion, your address changed and you were given a home you could never have afforded but whose mortgage has been paid in full. You now live in the gated community at the top of the hill because you're a different person in a different family after conversion. It is as if your very DNA has changed. At conversion, you are in the Son and are beloved to the Father.

Jesus gave us another analogy to help us understand how radical this transfer to being in Christ is. When God breathes spiritual life into a person upon conversion, the Holy Spirit performs a metaphorical heart surgery, giving her a new heart with redesigned loves and affections. God gives the person a regenerated nature that is so radically different from the old self that He calls the person a new creation. 'If anyone is in Christ, he is a new creation. The old has passed away; behold, the new has come' (2 Cor. 5:17). With this understanding, the language Jesus used with Nicodemus of being 'born again' (John 3:3) makes sense. As a new creation, we need a new birth. This isn't an improvement on our current life, but an entirely new one – found only in Christ.

Pictures of Union with Christ

Theologians often refer to our union with Christ as 'mystical' following the language of Paul, who called it a profound mystery (Eph. 5:32). But in His wisdom, God gave us several pictures to help us better understand our union with Christ. In fact, Scripture provides us with some rather ordinary illustrations to help us understand this glorious, cosmic union: a vine and its branches, a body with many parts, and a marriage between a man and a woman. As Creator of all things, God made these images so that we could better understand gospel truths.

A Vineyard Full of Grapes

Jesus is the vine; we are the branches. Jesus said, 'Abide in me, and I in you. As the branch cannot bear fruit by itself, unless it abides in the vine, neither can you, unless you abide in me. I am the vine; you are the branches. Whoever abides in me and I in him, he it is that bears much fruit, for apart from me you can do nothing' (John 15:4-5). These words, spoken by Jesus while He was still on earth, pointed to His future union with His blood-bought people. Branches receive nourishment and strength from a living vine, and as a result they produce fruit. (The fruit has seeds in order to produce even more fruit.) A branch separated from the vine is nothing more than a stick, useless to bear any fruit. Sticks are gathered up and thrown into the fire to burn (John 15:6). As long as the branch is connected to the vine, it receives sustenance and remains alive and fruitful. This life-giving connection is what it means to be united with Christ. Jesus is the vine; we are the branches. We receive nourishment from Christ who strengthens us and enables us to do the good works He has for us to do.

In fact, it is the fruit born in our lives that proves we are in Christ and brings glory to God. 'By this my Father is glorified, that you bear much fruit and so prove to be my disciples' (John 15:8). Sticks don't produce fruit; fruit only comes from branches connected to the vine. Therein lies a helpful test to see whether you are in Christ. Are you producing fruit?

Jesus helpfully explains a profound truth in this vine-branches analogy. He teaches us that the Father loves the Son, and likewise the Son loves those who are in Him. As we remain, or abide, in this place of being loved so perfectly (with the same love God has for His Son), our response is obedience to Him. 'As the Father has loved me, so have I loved you. Abide in my love. If you keep my commandments, you will abide in my love, just as I have kept my Father's commandments and abide in his love' (John 15:9-10). Our obedience is not the condition for Jesus' love; but it is the response we have to being loved. It is the fruit. If you are abiding, you are. Jesus obeyed His Father as He remained in His Father's perfect love. So we are to do the same. His love for us leads to obedience in us.

Remarkably, we find out this love and obedience sequence is for our pleasure. 'These things I have spoken to you, that my joy may be in you, and that your joy may be full' (John 15:11). Full joy is what God is extending in our union with Christ. Is there a pleasure greater or longer lasting than the full joy of Christ? Not a partial, temporary, or substandard joy, but full and eternal joy being offered by the author of it. As we abide in His love, the fruit of obedience follows in response. Imagine a vineyard full of grapes. Full joy from Christ results from our union with Him.

PHYSICALLY FIT

Jesus is the head of the body of Christ (Rom. 12:5, 1 Cor. 12:12-31, Eph. 3:6, Eph. 5:23, Col. 1:18, Col. 1:24). The interconnectedness of a body to its head helps us understand the mystical union of Christ and His people. The fingers on a hand are not disconnected from the arm, nose, or leg. And none act apart from the head. There is a unity among the parts of a body. When one part is in pain or broken, the other parts help. When everything is healthy, the parts of the body work together to accomplish the task given to it by the head. Even as I type these lines, my eyes are working to read the words, my fingers are coordinated in typing, my lungs are breathing in oxygen, and my heart is pumping blood to my organs. These parts are interconnected to each other and my brain gives the command to read, type, breathe and pump. My head gives the instructions and my body parts act according to the direction they have been given.

When Saul was traveling the Damascus road en route to persecute Christians, he was suddenly blinded by a bright light, and the voice of Jesus asked Saul, 'Why are you persecuting me?' (Acts 9:4). Because Jesus identified so closely with His church, He accused Saul of persecuting Him when Saul was harming them. To inflict harm on any members of the body of Christ is to inflict harm on Christ Himself.

The church is the body of Christ. The body analogy shows us that through Christ we are not only united vertically to our head, but we are also united horizontally to one another. 'In one Spirit, we were all baptized into one body' (1 Cor. 12:13). In the Garden of Gethsemane the night He was betrayed, Jesus prayed to the Father for His people to know unity with one another. '…for those who will believe in me … that that may all be one, just as you, Father, are in me, and I in you…' (John 17:20). Jesus specifically prayed for those who would one day believe in Him – you and me – to be unified with other people who are also in Christ. Remarkably, He asks for the same unity to be present in us as is in the Trinity. The fact that our unity with each other was on Jesus' mind as He faced His certain death means there is something significant to it. His prayer shows us that unity is important to Him and to us. And because He prayed for it, unity must not come naturally to us. We probably don't need any theological proof for that. My guess is you have plenty of empirical evidence to support that claim.

We need each other. As sinners plodding through this life, we need to link arms with other people who are committed to the same loves and have the same head. None of us are islands independent of each other. We need the encouragement that comes from one another. We need the love and the occasional rebuke that comes from one another. The forgiveness, admonition, and prayer that comes from knowing each other in community. We need to serve and be served by each other's gifts. This unity is a huge privilege to being united to Christ. These 'one another' relationships are most clearly seen in the local church, as people unite together under a shared faith and commit to loving each other, caring for one another, and holding one another accountable in the fight against sin. The way we love one another in unity displays the power of God in a manner that brings Him glory. When sinners are able to dwell in unity with one another, it is a supernatural gift and evidence of the work of the Holy Spirit. If your church knows unity, praise God for it. It brings Him glory. If your church is not currently experiencing unity, do your part to seek it. Pray for it. Humbly lay down your disagreements with others for the sake of your head and pursue unity with your brothers and sisters in Christ.

Jesus is the head; we are merely His body, acting in one accord and in deployment of His will.

A SPLENDID BRIDE

Jesus is the husband in another word picture of union with Christ. As two people are united in holy matrimony, they take on a new collective identity. Their happiness and sorrow are bound up in each other, and they take on a new responsibility for one another. Biblically, they are called 'one flesh' which describes their sexual union but encompasses so much more. They care for each other as they would for their own body. They no longer make decisions apart from the other. Their entire orientation in life has changed.

In His purposes for the world, God created marriage at the very beginning, even before the fall, so that when the gospel was revealed we would have a three-dimensional picture of it. Marriage is a small illustration that gives us a big picture understanding of our union with Christ. Paul tells wives to submit to their husbands because 'Now as the church submits to Christ, so also wives should submit in everything to their husbands' (Eph. 5:24). He tells husbands to love their wives 'as Christ loved the church and gave himself up for her that he might sanctify her, having cleansed her by the washing of water with the word, so that he might present the church to himself in splendor, without spot or wrinkle or any such thing, that she might be holy and without blemish' (Eph. 5:25-27). Our union with Christ is described as His sacrificial love for us and our submission to Him in response to that love.

Christ's sacrificial love for the church leads to her splendor. The church is spotless, without wrinkle, holy, and without blemish because of Christ's love and sacrifice for her. His work in cleansing His bride by the word leads to a collective holiness and beauty, a gift then presented back to Christ Himself. The way a husband is to love his wife should mirror that of Christ. He is to love and sacrifice for her as she is to respond to this love in submission to him.

Paul calls this union a mystery, meaning that it was once concealed but has now been revealed. The roles of the church and Christ are played by wives and husbands on a daily basis all around the world. If you are married, your marriage and those around you are a picture of the gospel, a living illustration of Christ and His bride being united as one. (Certainly, this is at least one reason there is such an attack on marriages: domineering or complacent husbands, controlling or complaining wives, infidelity and divorce. Satan would delight to destroy all the illustrations we have of this most blessed union of Christ and His people.) Jesus gently leads

His church, working in us by the preaching of His Word and the power of the Holy Spirit as we submit to Him and live under His protection and provision. Jesus is the husband; we are His bride.

Past, Present, and Future Realities

Our being bound up in Jesus means we share in the rights and privileges of community with the Father and the Spirit. We don't want to be merely a fan looking on from the sidelines; we want to be securely standing on the inside of this union communing with our God. For those who are in Christ, what is true for Him is true for us, even though we live thousands of years after He did and we likely live far away from the Galilean countryside where He ministered. Those who are in Christ identify with Him without the boundaries of time or place. Even though we are not living at the same time and in the same place as He lived and died, Scripture teaches that we were 'crucified with him' (Rom. 6:6, Gal. 2:20), 'buried with him' (Rom. 6:4), and were raised with Him (Col. 3:1). We also ascended with Him (Eph. 2:6) and will reign with Him (2 Tim. 2:12, Rom. 5:17, Eph. 2:6). Although mysterious, these statements tell us that we take part in Christ's death, burial, resurrection, ascension, and glorification 'in him'.

Spiritual Life

Paul taught, 'If anyone is in Christ, he is a new creation' (2 Cor. 5:17). Union of the believer to Christ means that our conversion from spiritual death to life is certain. When Jesus died on the cross, our old selves died with Him, and when He rose from the dead, we were raised to new life. Whether we feel like our faith is strong or weak is inconsequential to our salvation if we are in Christ. Our justification is not a religious experience with varying degrees of spiritual merit. One cannot be more in Christ than another. We have transferred our identity and we are a new creation. We've moved locations.

The transfer from being in Adam to being in Christ means we cannot be more beloved to God than we already are. How beloved is Jesus to God? That is a significant question if you are united to Christ. Because of your union to Christ, your relationship to God is as secure as that of Jesus. We have fellowship with the Father because Jesus does. There are not varying degrees of proximity to God, as we are sometimes tempted to think. We can grow in our communion with God, but never in our union with Him.

Just as Adam was the representative head of mankind, Jesus now represents those who are in Him. Adam sinned and in doing so led all of us into sin. Now, by Christ's obedience, 'many will be made righteous' (Rom. 5:19). This should give us great confidence that our salvation is secure. Once we are in Christ, we are in, no matter how strong or weak our faith may seem. All three of the astronauts aboard the Apollo 13 mission made it back to earth safely. Their emotional state and level of confidence in the NASA scientists to get them home did not cause them to arrive any sooner or more safely. Your faith is a gift that ushered you into the safety of Christ; the relative amount of faith you perceive you have, does not dictate your standing at all. Whether you travel in fear, worry, anxiety, or confidence has little bearing on your safe arrival to your eternal home. It has everything to do with where you are – safely in Christ – not in how strong or weak your faith seems. What matters is the object of our faith (Jesus), not the subjectivity of its relative strength. Realizing this can help us travel this life in confidence without fear, worry and anxiety that our faith is not enough.

Armed with the knowledge that we are in Christ, we can then approach the throne of God with confidence. 'There is therefore now no condemnation for those who are in Christ Jesus' (Rom. 8:1). If you are in Christ Jesus, go boldly before your Father. Confess sin, seek help, praise Him, eagerly petition Him for all your needs.

OUT OF THE SLUMS

Not only is your justification secured in Christ, but so is your growth in godliness as you fight temptations and sin in this world. Those who are in Christ still sin and will still desire feeding your flesh that poisonous fruit, the first bite of which tastes so sweet. But your sin does not define you or control you. You recognize the familiarity of sin and hear it calling your name, but when you are in Christ you don't live in that dark realm anymore. You can have confidence that you are being sanctified because your sinful nature died with Christ. 'We know that our old self was crucified with him in order that the body of sin might be brought to nothing, so that we would no longer be enslaved to sin. For one who has died has been set free from sin' (Rom. 6:6-7). Death has set you free from the bondage of sin. You can join with Christ and fight it.

We also have confidence in our growth toward godliness because we have been raised with Christ. 'If then you have been raised with Christ, seek the things that are above, where Christ is, seated at the right hand of God. Set your minds on things that are above, not the things that are on earth. For you have died, and your life is hidden with Christ in God' (Col. 3:1-3). This is a reality in which you can be confident. That's the basis for Paul's next sentence to the church at Colossae. 'Put to death therefore what is earthly in you: sexual immorality, impurity, passion, evil desire, and covetousness, which is idolatry' (Col. 3:5). Paul is not hoping the Christians there can muster up the willpower to fight sin. He reminds them of their union with Christ, and therefore, they can put to death their already dead old self. You no longer have to continue to live like you did in the slums with your old, sinful habits; you now have new desires to please God and a new ability to do so.

The New Testament is full of these indicative/imperative pairs. Because of who Jesus is and what He has done (indicative statements of fact), go fight sin and do good (imperative commands). We are not told to do good in order to earn favored status before God. But because we have the favored status of God, we are freed to love, serve, and sacrifice for others. Take as an example the indicative/imperative pairs we just read in Colossians 3:

> If you have been raised with Christ (indicative), seek the things that are above (imperative).

> When Christ who is your life appears, then you also will appear with him in glory. (Indicative) Put to death therefore what is earthly in you... (imperative)

The child of the monarch is a future monarch. Where I live, we call him the Crown Prince. It is a statement of fact that he will assume the throne when his father leaves it. From childhood, he spends time training to rule well, and he grows into the position of rule and authority. He is not preparing in case he will assume the role. His position is secure, even while he prepares for it. This is true for the Christian as well. We are securely in Christ, but we continue to train toward Godliness. One day our sanctification process will be complete, and our glory will be fully revealed and known. But until then we grow in Godliness because we know our future is certain. Because the imperatives are based on the indicatives, our sanctification is secure in Christ just as our justification is secure.

NAVIGATE SAFELY HOME

As we saw in the Biblical pictures of union with Christ, unity with Jesus means we have unity with one another as well. While there is an individual aspect to our being united with Christ – me in Him and Him in me – there is also a corporate aspect to it. There are no divisions based on worldly categories. And as we all stand underneath the cross and united in Christ, we are one (Gal. 3:28). This is what Jesus prayed the night before His crucifixion. That we may be one.

At my church in the Middle East, our membership includes people from dozens of different countries. Afghanistan and America.

Costa Rica and Canada. Nepal, Nigeria, and the Netherlands. Korea and Kazakhstan. Ireland and India. Ethiopia and Egypt. South Africa and Syria. Pakistan and the Philippines. We are from many different backgrounds. Our native languages are different. Our dress is different. We eat different kinds of food and decorate our homes in different ways. Some of us work hourly jobs. Some of us are heads of companies. From a worldly standpoint, there is not much that would bring us all together in one room, much less fill that room with love for one another week after week after week. And yet because we are united to Christ, we are united in Christ to one another.

The love displayed in our congregation in spite of our many differences highlights the supernatural work of the Holy Spirit in bringing unity to us. A Nepalese brother offered to disciple an American young man. They met until the one from Nepal had to return to his home country, so an Egyptian man picked up the mantle and continues to disciple the young man from the US. An American family has a university student from Nigeria living with them, and they regularly open their home for hospitality to university students and anyone else in need of a hot meal and an edifying conversation about their Savior. Recently a family from Syria in the church needed a place to live. They moved in with a family from the church. A college student from India also lived there, as well as a mom and daughter from the Philippines. We jokingly called the group the United Nations, but their love for one another was altogether different from anything the world knows. They did not unite around food, language, dress, backgrounds, political affiliation, or hobbies. No, their bonds were much deeper and more significant than those things. They united around a shared love for Christ.

The church is made up of those who have been brought into Christ, and through the body of Christ on earth we can safely navigate the depths of sorrow and hopes of joy in this life and prepare for the next. Church life together should be our linking arms in unity as we await our eternal glory. On that final day our eyes will be open to see the blessings of our union with Christ and we will adore Him and praise Him together, thankful to have been brought safely home.

C. S. Lewis wrote, '…the dullest most uninteresting person you can talk to may one day be a creature which, if you saw it now, you would be strongly tempted to worship.'[5] He continued, 'There are no ordinary people. You have never talked to a mere mortal. Nations, cultures, arts, civilizations – these are mortal, and their life is to ours as the life of a gnat. But it is immortals whom we joke with, work with, marry, snub, and exploit.'[6] Of all the things you see and interact with in a day, the only ones that will last are the people. God has promised an end to this world and all that is in it, but He has promised an eternity for those made in His image. For those in Christ, our eternity will be with God in heaven.

If you are in Christ, your eternity with God is secure. The only way God can break communion with you is if He excommunicates His Son. He is certainly not going to do that. So rest assured that one day your union with Christ will be consummated. You will have a new glorified body, like that of your Savior, and you will live in a new world. It will be like the first Garden, but so much better. God will dwell directly with us. And our souls will finally be at rest in a place where we will be unable to sin. Can you imagine what existence will be like when you do not battle your own sin or that of another?

> For the trumpet will sound, and the dead will be raised imperishable, and we shall be changed. For this perishable body

5   Lewis, *The Weight of Glory*, p. 45.

6   Ibid, p. 46.

must put on the imperishable, and this mortal body must put on immortality. When the perishable puts on the imperishable, and the mortal puts on immortality, then shall come to pass the saying that is written:

'Death is swallowed up in victory.'
'O death, where is your victory?
O death, where is your sting?' (1 Cor. 15:52-55)

No more suffering. No more pain. We will have good work to do in heaven. We will have direct access to God without need for a mediator. And we will know our Savior face to face. Our worship of Him will be more brilliant and joyful than ever. Now we know in part, but then we will know in full.

What do we do in the meantime? 'Therefore, my beloved brothers, be steadfast, immovable, always abounding in the work of the Lord, knowing that in the Lord your labor is not in vain' (1 Cor. 15:58). You are in. You have been accepted. You do not need to work toward higher status before God, for it has been given to you in Christ. Now you are free to work from that position. You don't have to live for this world's perks. You will be raised immortal. Live for the glory that is coming.

Eternally in the Hands of God

As we have observed, being united with Christ means that we have an intimate, inseparable union with Christ that God gives us at salvation. This relationship is a work of God. That's why Paul wrote, 'because of him [God] you are in Christ Jesus' (1 Cor. 1:30). Once we have entered through the doors of faith into a relationship with our Lord, Christ promises us safety there. In Christ we have protection from Satan and the assurance that God will never let us go. In speaking about the security of His people, Jesus told the Jews, 'My Father, who has given them to me, is greater than all, and no one is able to snatch them out of the Father's hand' (John 10:29).

Is there any safer place to be than securely in the hands of God, who promises never to let go? If we are in Christ, we can be sure that the One who loves us and gave Himself for us will hold tightly to us.

> For my life He bled and died, Christ will hold me fast;
> Justice has been satisfied; He will hold me fast.
> Raised with Him to endless life, He will hold me fast
> 'Till our faith is turned to sight, When He comes at last!
>
> He will hold me fast, He will hold me fast;
> For my Savior loves me so, He will hold me fast.[7]

---

7   'He Will Hold Me Fast', Ada Habershon, 1906.

QUESTIONS

PERFECT ENDING

Union with Christ is a doctrine that teaches us what is true for Jesus is true for those who have been united to Him by faith. At salvation, we do not merely get the benefits offered from reconciliation with God, but we get Jesus Himself. Our union with Him is eternally secure, affecting not only our salvation but also our sanctification and glorification. Its end goal is our joy in having obtained Christ Himself.

1. How can finding her identity in Christ cause Stephanie (p. 233) to feel confident in the situation in which the Lord has placed her?

2. The Bible rarely uses the term 'Christian' but often uses the phrase 'in Christ' to describe those who have been regenerated. Being 'in Christ' is more significant than following Him or being His disciple. It means whatever is true for Him is true for us. Being 'in' communicates a positional relationship and intimacy. Using a concordance or online Bible, search for 'in Christ' and write down some of the various ways our relationship with the Lord is described.

3. Paul wrote to the church at Corinth, 'If anyone is in Christ, he is a new creation.' At regeneration, the new believer is given a new heart and a new standing in the world and before God – in Christ.

    a. How should the truth of this doctrine affect your identity?

    b. How does it affect the security of your salvation?

    c. How should it affect your sanctification?

    d. How does it give you hope in your future glorification?

4. What do we learn about union with Christ from each of the following pictures?

    a. A Vineyard

    b. A Body

    c. A Marriage

5. How is life in a local church affected by the doctrine of union with Christ?

6. Are you 'in' Christ? How can you be certain of your standing with Him? What are some of the tests given in Scripture to be certain of your right standing with God?

7. Paul wrote in Galatians, 'It is no longer I who live, but Christ who lives in me.' What does this verse mean? How do we intentionally seek to decrease so that Christ may increase in our lives?

Conclusion

When I agreed to write this book, I was a busy homeschool mom, married to a church planter, living overseas in the middle of a church construction project. We were raising three small children, and it was not exactly a season for quiet contemplation and reflective writing. But my excitement over the concept of a series of doctrinal books written by women for women led me to jump at the invitation to write, knowing I would first get to dig deeply into the doctrine of Christ myself. As I dug, I uncovered jewels and treasures that I could never put a price tag on. I hope some of what I found so beautiful about Christ and His work has shown in this book. By the time this book is published, my oldest child will be nearly a teenager and my fifth child will be celebrating his second birthday. While it has not been a season of quiet reflection, it has been a (rather extended) season of deep encouragement and growth for me personally, as I have come to know and love my Savior more because of who He is and what He has done. I know more firmly now than ever that our doctrine of Christ deeply affects our life. Our joys, our parenting, our marriages, our trials – are all directly influenced by what we believe about the Son of God.

Christology is not a topic to be studied apart from life. It isn't a doctrine to be shelved that we need to blow the dust off in order to study in a quiet library somewhere. As I came to a fresh understanding of different aspects of Jesus' person and work, I immediately found it applicable to my life and those around me. As I ministered to a friend suffering from depression and anxiety, I could speak about our union with Christ and that her hope is secure. Jesus has promised to never leave her. As I have grieved the sudden health decline of my father-in-law, I have taken comfort in the knowledge that his sins have been atoned for, and that Jesus is interceding even now for his every need. If Jesus has given His own life, is there anything good that He would withhold now? My father-in-law has no reason to fear the future, either in life or death. Just this week as I spoke with a friend who is healing from a traumatic situation, I reminded her that our Savior is not a far-away nameless deity, but that He became one of us and has experienced a physical life with its pain and limitations and temptations, just as we have. He was 'tempted in every way we are.' (Heb. 4:15) He is 'acquainted with all my ways.' (Ps. 139:3) Her intercessor is not unaware of the pain she is experiencing. He is praying for her with the acute awareness of what she is going through and the full knowledge of what she needs to heal.

My study of the person and work of Christ has shaped my parenting, the way I love my husband, the manner with which I seek contentment, and the vigor with which I serve my church. Seeing the story of Christ woven throughout all of Scripture has caused me to treasure time in His Word more deeply. Knowing the security of my salvation has strengthened my prayer life. I am motivated to pray bolder, bigger prayers to God because of my confidence that they reach His throne. In fact, it seems every aspect of life has been touched by my deeper understanding of Christ. This knowledge is essential for the joy-filled Christian life. J. I. Packer wrote, 'Christology is the true hub round which the wheel of theology revolves, and to which its separate spokes must each be correctly anchored if the wheel is not to get bent.'[1] If we get our theology of Christ wrong, our understanding of all other doctrines of God will be adversely affected.

But when we get our theology of Christ right, our worship of Him increases. We will praise Jesus in and for eternity because we will see Him clearly. When our faith turns to sight and we can touch the wounds of Jesus like Thomas did, we too will worship Him. Eternity will not be too long to praise the One who has given us eternal life.

---

1   J. I. Packer, 'Jesus Christ is Lord,' in *The J. I. Packer Collection*, comp. Alister McGrath (Downers Grove, IL: InterVarsity Press, 1999), p. 151.

Acknowledgements

I must first thank Keri Folmar for the opportunity she gave me to write and the graciousness and patience she showed me with each missed deadline. Keri, I am indebted to you for the ways you have mentored me and the opportunities you have given me. I praise God for you and John and the bushels of fruit born out of your years of faithful ministry.

A hearty thank you also to the truly lovely people at Christian Focus. May God continue to bless your good work! Thanks especially to Kate, Rosanna, and Anne. Your patience is a virtue.

Carrie Sandom, your advice was timely and helpful. I hope the book is better and more relevant to more women because of your insight. Thank you!

I also want to thank the women of RAK Evangelical Church. You are a blessing beyond measure to me! Thank you for caring so well for me and my family during busy seasons. Only the Lord knows how deeply encouraged I have been by the meals, prayers, and hours you spent babysitting. I especially want to thank the Wednesday morning women's Bible study who plowed through this material early on, challenging me, encouraging me, and praising Jesus with me. You are strong, joyful, theologically-driven women, and you have sharpened me. Thank you also to those who read parts of the first and roughest chapters of this book: Becky, Stephanie, Caleb, Carey, and Karen.

I expect extra jewels in your crowns in heaven for your heavy-lifting. I must also thank Marni, Jess, Julia and Sascha, Amanda and Jordan, and Jenia. You all know the costly and countless ways you have loved and served me and my family and how deeply grateful we are. If it were not for Arlene Yunson, this book never would have made it to print. I pray this book helps answer years of your praying for more understanding.

In God's providence, several really smart theologians came to visit us during the time I was writing. Thank you to Dr. Tom Schreiner, Dr. Steve Wellum, and Dr. Ligon Duncan for patiently talking through some of my questions. Each of you helped answer a pressing question I had at the time, and I am grateful for your insight.

I heartily thank my family for the many ways you have helped along the way. My parents first taught me the fundamental truth that I am still pondering today: Jesus loves me this I know, for the Bible tells me so. I was fortunate to grow up in a home that taught me to honor God with my life, by looking for opportunities and taking risks. Writing this book was certainly born from your shepherding of me in these ways. Thank you, Mom and Dad, for your sacrificial love for me and instilling in me the truth of the Gospel from a young age. My 'mother-in-love' Tony has prayed for me and has demonstrated what it means to abide in Christ. I have learned from your words and even more from your life. Thank you to my children, who have been anxiously waiting for me to be finished. We have many movie nights and hours at the beach to catch up on! Thank you to my husband Josh. You are my pastor, resident theologian, counselor, comedian, and my best friend. Thank you for not letting me quit, even though I declared hundreds of times I needed to. I have said it privately, but it bears repeating publicly: I know Jesus better because of the way you have loved me.

Finally, my ultimate gratitude is to God. I have been reminded each day that I studied and worked on this book that my salvation is a gift from you. I have nothing to boast about in my own strength.

My only boasting is in you and the lavish grace and love you have bestowed on me. You have brought a poor vile sinner into your house of wine, and you have given me the greatest gift of all: yourself.

> The bride eyes not her garment,
> But her dear bridegroom's face;
> I will not gaze at glory,
> But on my King of grace.
> Not at the crown he giveth
> But on his pierced hand;
> The Lamb is all the glory
> Of Emmanuel's land[1]

---

1 'Oh! Christ He is the Fountain', Anne Ross Cousin.

Selected Bibliography

Books about the atonement

St. Anselm. *Cur Deus Homo.* (Fort Worth, Texas: RDMc Publishing) Translated from the Latin by Sidney Norton Deane (B.A. Chicago: The Open Court Publishing Company, 1903 edition)

Aulén, Gustav. (transl. by A.G. Herbert SSM) *Christus Victor: An Historical Study of the Three Main Types of the Idea of Atonement* (London: SPCK, 1931; New York City: Macmillan, 1969)

Dever, Mark and Lawrence, Michael. *It is Well: Expositions on Substitutionary Atonement (9Marks)* (Wheaton, Illinois: Crossway, 2010)

Gibson, David and Gibson, Jonathan (editors). *From Heaven He Came and Sought Her: Definite Atonement in Historical, Biblical, Theological, and Pastoral Perspective* (Wheaton, Illinois: Crossway, 2013)

Jeffrey, Steve; Ovey, Michael; and Sach, Andrew. *Pierced for our Transgression: Rediscovering the Glory of Penal Substitution* (Wheaton, Illinois: Crossway 2007)

Kempis, Thomas à. (trans. George F. Maine. 1441) *The Imitation of Christ* (London: Collins, 1957)

Macleod, Donald. *Christ Crucified: Understanding the Atonement* (Downers Grove, Illinois: IVP Academic, 2014)

Morris, Leon. *The Atonement: Its Meaning and Significance* (Downers Grove, Illinois: IVP Academic 1984)

Packer, J. I. and Dever, Mark. *In My Place Condemned He Stood: Celebrating the Glory of the Atonement* (Wheaton, Illinois: Crossway 2009)

Stott, John R. W. *The Cross of Christ* (London: IVP, 1986)

Biblical Theology

Beale, G. K. *A New Testament Biblical Theology: The Unfolding of the Old Testament in the New* (Grand Rapids, Michigan: Baker Academic, 2011)

Gentry, Peter J. *Kingdom Through Covenant: A Biblical-Theological Understanding of the Covenants* (Wheaton, Illinois: Crossway, 2012)

Goldsworthy, Graeme. *The Gospel and Kingdom* (Milton Keyes, England: Paternoster, 2012)

Hamilton, Jr., James M. *God's Glory in Salvation Through Judgement: A Biblical Theology* (Wheaton, Illinois: Crossway, 2010)

Schreiner, Thomas R. *New Testament Theology: Magnifying God in Christ* (Grand Rapids, Michigan: Baker Academic, 2008)

Christology and books about Jesus

Bailey, Kenneth E. *Jesus Through Middle Eastern Eyes: Cultural Studies in the Gospels* (Downers Grove, Illinois: IVP Academic, 2008)

Bock, Darrell L. *Jesus According to Scripture: Restoring the Portrait from the Gospels* (Grand Rapids, Michigan: Baker Academic, 1990)

Brown, Archibald. *The Face of Jesus Christ: The Person and Work of our Lord* (Carlisle, Pennsylvania: Banner of Truth, 2012)

Carson, D. A. *Christ and Culture Revisited* (Grand Rapids, Michigan: Eerdmans, 2008)

Carson, D. A. *Jesus the Son of God: A Christological Title Often Overlooked, Sometimes Misunderstood, and Currently Disputed* (Wheaton, Illinois: Crossway, 2012)

Carson, D. A. *The Scriptures Testify about Me: Jesus and the Gospel in the Old Testament* (Wheaton, Illinois: Crossway, 2013)

Clowney, Edmund P. *The Unfolding Mystery: Discovering Christ in the Old Testament* (Phillipsburg, New Jersey: Presbyterian and Reformed Publishing Company, 1991)

Demarest, Bruce. *The Cross and Salvation: The Doctrine of Salvation (Foundations of Evangelical Theology)* (Wheaton, Illinois: Crossway, 2006)

Eswine, Zack. *Sensing Jesus: Life and Ministry as a Human Being* (Wheaton, Illinois: Crossway, 2012)

Ferguson, Sinclair B. *The Christian Life: A Doctrinal Introduction* (Carlisle, Pennsylvania: Banner of Truth, 1981)

Ferguson, Sinclair B. *The Whole Christ: Legalism, Antinomianism, and Gospel Assurance – Why the Marrow Controversy Still Matters* (Wheaton, Illinois: Crossway, 2016)

Gilbert, Greg. *Who is Jesus? (9Marks)* (Wheaton, Illinois: Crossway, 2015)

Letham, Robert. *The Work of Christ (Contours of Christian Theology)* (Downers Grove, Illinois: IVP Academic, 1993)

Macleod, Donald. *The Person of Christ (Contours of Christian Theology)* (Downers Grove, Illinois: IVP Academic, 1998)

Morgan, Christopher and Peterson, Robert A. (Editors). Bray, Gerald (contributor) *The Deity of Christ* (Wheaton, Illinois: Crossway, 2011)

Owen, John. *The Glory of Christ (Puritan Paperbacks: Treasures of John Owen for Today's Readers)* (Carlisle, Pennsylvania: Banner of Truth, 1994)

Packer, J.I. *Growing in Christ* (Wheaton, Illinois: Crossway, 2007)

Piper, John. *Counted Righteous in Christ* (Wheaton, Illinois: Crossway, 2002)

Piper, John. *Fifty Reasons Why Jesus Came to Die* (Wheaton, Illinois: Crossway, 2006)

Piper, John. *What Jesus Demands from the World* (Wheaton, Illinois: Crossway, 2006)

Reeves, Michael. *Christ Our Life* (Milton Keyes, United Kingdom: Paternoster Press, 2014)

Sanders, J. Oswald. *The Incomparable Christ (Moody Classics)* (Chicago, Illinois: Moody Publishers, 2009 Edition: New Edition)

Schreiner, Thomas R. *Magnifying God in Christ: A Summary of New Testament Theology* (Grand Rapids, Michigan: Baker Academic, 2010)

Sproul. R.C. *The Truth of the Cross* (Sanford, Florida: Reformation Trust Publishing, 2007)

Stott, John R. W. *The Incomparable Christ* (London: IVP, 2001)

Strauss, Mark L. *Four Portraits, One Jesus: A Survey of Jesus and the Gospels* (Grand Rapids, Michigan: Zondervan, 2007)

Ware, Bruce. *The Man Christ Jesus: Theological Reflections on the Humanity of Christ* (Wheaton, Illinois: Crossway, 2012)

Wellum, Stephen J. *Christ Alone – The Uniqueness of Jesus as Savior: What the Reformers Taught…and Why It Still Matters (The Five Solas Series)* (Grand Rapids, Michigan: Zondervan 2017)

Wellum, Stephen J. *God the Son Incarnate: The Doctrine of Christ (Foundations of Evangelical Theology)* (Wheaton, Illinois: Crossway, 2016)

Systematic Theology

Bavinck, Herman. *Reformed Dogmatics, Volume 3: Sin and Salvation in Christ* (Grand Rapids, Michigan: Baker Academic, 2006)

Berkhof, Louis. *Systematic Theology* (Grand Rapids, Michigan: Eerdmans, 1996, first edition)

Calvin, John. *Institutes of the Christian Religion,* II.xvi (ed. J. T. McNeill; trans. F. L. Battles; Philadelphia: Westminster, 1960)

Erickson, Miller. *Christian Theology* (Grand Rapids, Michigan: Baker Academic, 2013)

Feinberg, John S. *No One Like Him: The Doctrine of God Foundations of Evangelical Theology* (Wheaton, Illinois: Crossway, 2006)

Frame, John M. *Systematic Theology: An Introduction to Christian Belief* (Phillipsburg, New Jersey: P&R Publishing, 2013)

Frame, John M. *Salvation Belongs to the Lord: An Introduction to Systematic Theology* (Phillipsburg, New Jersey: P&R Publishing, 2006)

Grudem, Wayne. *Systematic Theology: An Introduction to Biblical Doctrine* (Leicester, England: IVP and Grand Rapids Michigan: Zondervan, 1994)

Reeves, Michael. *Delighting in the Trinity: An Introduction to the Christian Faith* (Downers Grove, Illinois: IVP Academic, 2012)

Schreiner, Thomas R. *The King in His Beauty: A Biblical Theology of the Old and New Testaments* (Grand Rapids, Michigan: Baker Academic, 2013)

Van Til, Cornelius. *Christian Apologetics* (Phillipsburg, New Jersey: P&R Publishing, 2003)

Other Books

Demarest, Bruce. *The Cross and Salvation* (Wheaton, Illinois: Crossway, 2006)

Lewis, C. S. *Mere Christianity* from the *Complete C. S. Lewis Signature Classics* (C. S. Lewis Pte. Ltd. 1952)

Packer, J. I. *Knowing God* (London: IVP, 1993)

Pink, A. W. *Spiritual Union and Communion* (Grand Rapids: Baker Publishing, 1971)

Schreiner, Thomas. *Faith Alone: The Doctrine of Justification* (Grand Rapids, Michigan: Zondervan, 2015)

Sproul, R. C. *The Holiness of God* (Carol Stream, Illinois: Tyndale House 1998, second edition)

Wilcox, Jeffrey A., Tice, Terrence N., and Kelsey, Catherine L. (eds.) *Schleiermacher's Influences on American Thought and Religious* Life (1835-1920), *Volume One* (Eugene, Oregon: Pickwick Publications 2013)

Articles

West, Aaron J. 'Arius – Thalia in Greek and English'. Fourth Century Christianity. Wisconsin Lutheran College. Retrieved 16 August 2016.

http://www.apuritansmind.com/creeds-and-confessions/the-chalcedonian-creed-circa-451-a-d/

IX Marks journal. Phil Ryken. https://www.9marks.org/article/praying-as-a-church-for-the-world-and-your-city/ June 21, 2016.

Sermons

Sinclair B. Ferguson, 2011 Ligonier National Conference, Light & Heat: A Passion for the Holiness of God. 'Why the God-Man.'

https://www.desiringgod.org/messages/jesus-christ-is-an-advocate-for-sinners

Sermon at Bethlehem Baptist Church on Romans 4:22-25, October 3, 1999. https://www.desiringgod.org/messages/why-was-jesus-put-to-death-and-raised-again

John Piper, sermon, 2014 Desiring God conference, Feb 3, 2014

Scripture Index

THE GOOD PORTION:

Scripture

The Doctrine of Scripture for Every Woman

KERI FOLMAR

The Good Portion — Scripture

The Doctrine of Scripture for Every Woman

Keri Folmar

The Bible speaks about itself in evocative language – a light to the path, a balm to the flesh, sweeter than honey. It is more than a formula – it is the heartbeat of a Christian. This first title in *The Good Portion* series addresses the nature of the Scriptures as God's revelation and discusses the characteristics of the Bible.

If you're frustrated with fluff and longing to learn, The Good Portion is for you. Please read this book-it's a treasure chest full of wisdom that will help you delight in the riches of God's Word.

Melissa B. Kruger

Conference speaker, Women's Ministry Coordinator, Uptown Church, Charlotte, North Carolina

978-1-7819-1978-1

THE GOOD PORTION:

God

The Doctrine of God
for Every Woman

REBECCA STARK

SERIES EDITOR: KERI FOLMAR

The Good Portion: God

The Doctrine of God for Every Woman

Rebecca Stark

God has revealed Himself to us in His Word. As we study what He says about Himself, and see more of His perfection, worth, magnificence and beauty, we glimpse His glory. This second title in *The Good Portion* series looks at what the Bible says about God – Father, Son and Holy Spirit – that we might know Him better and glorify Him.

Rebecca Stark presents to us a robust introduction into theology that will lead the reader to adore, delight in, and praise God for who he is and what he has done.

Aimee Byrd

Author of *Housewife Theologian, Theological Fitness*, and *No Little Women*

978-1-5271-0111-1

Christian Focus Publications

Our mission statement —

STAYING FAITHFUL

In dependence upon God we seek to impact the world through literature faithful to His infallible Word, the Bible. Our aim is to ensure that the Lord Jesus Christ is presented as the only hope to obtain forgiveness of sin, live a useful life and look forward to heaven with Him.

Our Books are published in four imprints:

CHRISTIAN FOCUS

popular works including biographies, commentaries, basic doctrine and Christian living.

CHRISTIAN HERITAGE

books representing some of the best material from the rich heritage of the church.

MENTOR

books written at a level suitable for Bible College and seminary students, pastors, and other serious readers. The imprint includes commentaries, doctrinal studies, examination of current issues and church history.

CF4•K

children's books for quality Bible teaching and for all age groups: Sunday school curriculum, puzzle and activity books; personal and family devotional titles, biographies and inspirational stories – Because you are never too young to know Jesus!

Christian Focus Publications Ltd,
Geanies House, Fearn, Ross-shire,
IV20 1TW, Scotland, United Kingdom.
www.christianfocus.com